Albie Sachs
26/6/08

The Strange Alchemy of Life and Law

The Strange Alchemy
of Life and Law

•

JUSTICE ALBIE SACHS

OXFORD
UNIVERSITY PRESS

OXFORD
UNIVERSITY PRESS

Great Clarendon Street, Oxford OX2 6DP

Oxford University Press is a department of the University of Oxford.
It furthers the University's objective of excellence in research, scholarship,
and education by publishing worldwide in

Oxford New York

Auckland Cape Town Dar es Salaam Hong Kong Karachi
Kuala Lumpur Madrid Melbourne Mexico City Nairobi
New Delhi Shanghai Taipei Toronto

With offices in

Argentina Austria Brazil Chile Czech Republic France Greece
Guatemala Hungary Italy Japan Poland Portugal Singapore
South Korea Switzerland Thailand Turkey Ukraine Vietnam

Oxford is a registered trade mark of Oxford University Press
in the UK and in certain other countries

Published in the United States
by Oxford University Press Inc., New York

British Library Cataloguing in Publication Data

Data available

Library of Congress Cataloging in Publication Data

Data available

Typeset by Newgen Imaging Systems (P) Ltd., Chennai, India
Printed in Great Britain
on acid-free paper by
Clays Ltd, St Ives plc

ISBN 978–0–19–957179–6

1 3 5 7 9 10 8 6 4 2

The lovely little boy that Vanessa and I brought into the world two years ago has to our delight just used the word 'why?' If one day he wants to know why we named him Oliver, why his Daddy has one arm, and why his Daddy is called a Judge, he can find the answers in this book.

About the Author

On turning six, during World War II, Albie Sachs received a card from his father expressing the wish that he would grow up to be a soldier in the fight for liberation.

His career in human rights activism started at the age of 17, when as a second year law student at the University of Cape Town, he took part in the Defiance of Unjust Laws Campaign. Three years later he attended the Congress of the People at Kliptown where the Freedom Charter was adopted. He started practice as an advocate at the Cape Bar aged 21. The bulk of his work involved defending people charged under racist statutes and repressive security laws. He himself was raided by the security police, subjected to banning orders restricting his movement and eventually placed in solitary confinement for two prolonged spells of detention.

In 1966 he went into exile. After spending eleven years doing a doctorate at Sussex and teaching law at Southampton he worked for a further eleven years in Mozambique as law professor and legal researcher. In 1988 he was seriously injured by a bomb placed in his car by South African security agents, losing an arm and the sight of an eye.

During the 1980s working closely with Oliver Tambo, leader of the ANC in exile, he helped draft the organization's Code of Conduct, as well as its statutes. Once he had returned to health after the car bomb, he devoted himself to preparations for a new democratic Constitution for South Africa. In 1990 he returned home and as a member of the Constitutional Committee and the National Executive of the ANC took part in the negotiations which led to South Africa becoming a constitutional democracy. After the first democratic election in 1994 he was appointed by President Nelson Mandela to serve on the newly established Constitutional Court.

He has travelled to many countries sharing South African experience in healing divided societies, been engaged in the sphere of art and architecture, and played an active role in the development of the Constitutional Court building and its art collection on the site of the Old Fort Prison in Johannesburg. Author of many books, his Jail Diary was dramatized for the Royal Shakespeare Company and broadcast by the BBC.

Honorary Bencher of Lincoln's Inn, he is an Appeals Commissioner of the International Cricket Council.

Justice Albie Sachs delivering the judgment in *Fourie*, the *Same Sex Marriages* case, Chapter 9

Judith Mason, *The Man Who Sang and the Woman Who
Kept Silent 2*, 1995

The Man Who Sang and the Woman Who Kept Silent

The work on the cover of this book commemorates the courage of Phila Ndwandwe and Harald Sefola whose deaths during the Struggle were described to the Truth and Reconciliation Commission by their killers.

Phila Ndwandwe was shot by the security police after being kept naked for weeks in an attempt to make her inform on her comrades. She preserved her dignity by making panties out of a blue plastic bag. This garment was found wrapped around her pelvis when she was exhumed. 'She simply would not talk', one of the policeman involved in her death testified. 'God...she was brave.'

Harald Sefola was electrocuted with two comrades in a field outside Witbank. While waiting to die he requested to sing *Nkosi Sikelel' iAfrika*. His killer recalled, 'he was a very brave man who believed strongly in what he was doing.'

I wept when I heard Phila's story, saying to myself, 'I wish I could make you a *dress*.' Acting on this childlike response, I collected discarded blue plastic bags that I sewed into a dress. On its skirt I painted this letter:

Sister, a plastic bag may not be the whole armour of God, but you were wrestling with flesh and blood, and against powers, against the rulers of darkness, against spiritual wickedness in sordid places. Your weapons were your silence and a piece of rubbish. Finding that bag and wearing it until you were disinterred is such a frugal, commonsensical, house-wifely thing to do, an ordinary act…At some level you shamed your captors, and they did not compound their abuse of you by stripping you a second time. Yet they killed you. We only know your story because a sniggering man remembered how brave you were. Memorials to your courage are everywhere; they blow about in the streets and drift on the tide and cling to thorn-bushes. This dress is made from some of them. *Hambe kahle. Umkhonto.*

The dress, swinging on its hanger in the breeze, reminded me of the drapery on the *Victory of Samothrace* in the Louvre. So I painted a local Victory figure moving through imprisoning grids of wire accompanied by a hyena—at once a predator and a scavenger.

Justice Albie Sachs saw these pieces and a painting of three braziers I had made in memory of Sefola and his friends. He suggested I combine Phila's dress and the braziers into a commemorative work. Eventually the dress, the dress painting, and the second larger canvas were all placed together in the South African Constitutional Court.

Having the opportunity to honour the man who sang and the woman who kept silent has been a privilege, but it leaves me with an abiding sense of shame.

Judith Mason

Preface

This book should be of huge interest to the international judicial community and everyone else who is interested in justice. It gives a rare insight into Albie Sachs' unique approach to justice. Anybody of the many people who, like myself, have had the privilege of spending time in his company or listened to him giving lectures, will find his personal qualities leaping out of every page. However, it is those judges (not all judges) who believe judging is much more than merely deciding cases who will obtain the greatest benefit and pleasure from what he has written.

If I still had responsibility for the English judiciary, I would encourage every judge for whom I was responsible to read it. I am sure it would improve their understanding of what the job really involves and what justice is about.

Of course, not everyone will agree with his views on some of the issues he considers but certainly in this country an increasing proportion of the judiciary would do so. Issues such as same sex marriage are highly controversial and that is why in the more conservative UK we leave them to Parliament in so far as we can. However, sometimes Parliament is not prepared to do the job for us and then we, as judges, have to do our best in the culture in which we work to fill the gaps that are left.

Albie Sachs has a gift, which unfortunately is one which is shared by few others, of expressing complex issues with simplicity and clarity. This does not mean, as he makes clear, that he does not have to struggle to set out his conclusions.

Personally, I am in sympathy with almost everything he has to say. There was one small issue on which I thought he was absolutely right, which was the question of damages for defamation. As he knows, damages, especially if you are a celebrity, can be extraordinarily large here. This is wholly out of proportion with the modest damages you receive for fatal injuries. As the book makes clear, what is essential is an apology, though sometimes generous compensation has a beneficial effect on irresponsible conduct on the part of the media.

This is an important book and I welcome its publication.

Harry Woolf
Formerly Lord Chief Justice of England, Wales and Northern Ireland
London: December 2008

Acknowledgements

Chapter Four draws in part on Cardozo Law Review, 'Reason, Passion, and "The Progress of Law"', Brennan, William J, Jr (Vol 10, October/November 1988).

Chapter Five includes extracts from *The Soft Vengeance of a Freedom Fighter*, Albie Sachs (2nd edn, Cape Town: David Philip; Berkeley: University of California Press, 2000, first published in 1990 in Great Britain by Grafton Books), pp 9–12 and 116–119.

Contents

Prologue

L ife prepared me in a most bizarre way for becoming a judge. If judicial office had been my goal I was doing everything right... eight years of study and three degrees including a doctorate in law, a decade of busy practice as an advocate at the Cape Town Bar, and, later, earnestly teaching law in three continents and publishing several books, some scholarly, others autobiographical. Yet as far as the actual impact of the law on my life was concerned, everything was wrong: as a student my home was raided before dawn by the police and I was subjected to what was called a 'banning order' that restricted my movements and activities; while at the Bar I was twice placed in solitary confinement by the security police, first for 168 days and later for 3 months, during which I suffered torture by sleep deprivation; when I completed my doctorate I was living as a stateless person in exile in England; and some years later while doing legal research in Mozambique I was blown up by a bomb placed in my car by my country's security agents, losing an arm and the sight of an eye.

The fact is that for much of my life I lived simultaneously as lawyer and as outlaw. Anyone who has been in clandestinity will know how split the psyche becomes when you work through the law in the public sphere, and against the law in the underground. Yet the causes were easy to understand and the resolution as obvious to predict—only when we ended apartheid and realigned the law with justice, could I become whole again. Less dangerous but more disturbing was a deeper disquiet at the centre of my legal soul, one that was aggravated by the grotesqueries of apartheid, but that had a more profound and more problematic genesis.

I first became aware of it when I was a student at the University of Cape Town. The sun streamed into our lecture rooms as I listened dutifully to professors speaking on what I have since heard described as the beautiful abstraction of norms. To pass exams I would repeat elegant textbook phrases about the rule of law, basic rights and the independence of the judiciary. Then at night, in a shack lit by flickering candles, I would conduct study classes and see the expressive eyes and mouths of desperately poor people incandescent with determination to give all their energies, even their lives, for justice and freedom. I would be deeply animated by a vitality and laughter that seemed vastly more meaningful for the achievement of justice than any of the erudite but passionless phrases of my law school. Two worlds in the same city, yet totally apart, joined by pain rather than by hope, and I did not live completely in either.

For more than thirty years of my life as a lawyer I battled with this divided self. Unexpectedly, it was the bomb that blasted the schism away. The bomb literally hurled me out of my legal routine, and freed me to recreate my life from the beginning. I learnt to walk, to stand, to run...and to prepare for the writing of South Africa's new Constitution. Suddenly, joyously and voluptuously, the grand abstract phrases of the legal text books united with and embraced the palpable passion for justice of the disenfranchised. And far from the law constituting a barricade of injustice that had to be stormed and torn down for freedom to be achieved, it became a primary instrument for accomplishing peaceful revolution. In the months and years of constitution-making that followed, the formerly contradictory influences of my life were able to synergise. If the process of making of a new basic law helped my country to heal itself, it also resolved my own deep internal contradiction.

And so it came to pass that if some people are born to be judges and some achieve judicial office, I was one of those that had judicial office happily thrust upon him. And what extraordinarily rich and intellectually exciting years have passed since the day fourteen years ago when newly-elected President Nelson Mandela appointed me and ten colleagues as members of South Africa's first Constitutional Court.

I never took my being a judge as something natural, preordained, and unproblematic. The intensely contradictory nature of my earlier relationship to the law would not have allowed this. Furthermore, being involved in socio-legal studies in my years of exile led one to observe and interrogate what I and my colleagues were actually doing. And then I was constantly being pressed by universities and legal groups throughout the world to explain what they saw as the miracle of the establishment of a constitutional democracy in a country destined for a racial bloodbath. If you want to give credit to the miraculous without believing in miracles, you are compelled to search with particular diligence for rational explanations. How did the transition take place, and what role was I now playing as a judge?

I found myself giving presentations all over the globe on questions that were raising similar controversies in the most varied jurisdictions. The lectures, repeated over the years in places as far apart as New York, London, Delhi, Cambridge and Chicago, were collected for a possible book of essays. The bundle lacked connecting texture, so to add some starch I began to mix in extracts from judgments that had been delivered in my Court, some by myself, some by colleagues. At the very least this would show an interesting contrast between the more accessible and personalized cadences of a lecture, and the oracular and disinterested voice of a judgment. I noticed, however, that the compare-and-contrast effect of conjoining narrative text with judgment excerpts was beginning to provide my imagination with something more exciting—glimpses of a fascinating and not very obvious chemistry between my non-judicial life experiences and my decision-making as a judge. And in this way a totally new book began to construct itself within the innards of the manuscript.

The most dramatic experiences in my life involved terrorism and torture. A simple response to my past would have been to show unrelenting opposition to those who had engaged in the grossly inhuman practices of the apartheid era. How, I could have asked, could people who had mercilessly set out to negate the right to equality and right to a fair trial, now seek to benefit from the very concepts they had sought to? I had been deemed a terrorist, had fought against the use of terrorism as a weapon in the freedom struggle, had had to deal with torture employed against agents sent to destroy the liberation organization to which I belonged, and had been the victim of state terrorism. Yet, looking back at my judicial texts, it became clear that my responses from the bench had turned out to be far more complex. Life experiences had undoubtedly seeped into my judicial vision, but always through the prism of established and evolving principles of legal thought.

My biggest surprise in preparing this book came with the section dealing with my relationship with the Truth and Reconciliation Commission (TRC), which happened to include meeting with the operative who had organized the placing of the bomb in my car. I had thought that my TRC experience had been totally divorced from my thinking as a judge. Yet going through my judgments, I realized that the theme of reconciliation had lodged itself deeply into my legal consciousness, surfacing rather strongly in two of them. One emphasized the role of apology as a restorative justice response to defamation (libel). The other stressed the role of mediation in reconciling the rights of poor landless people with those of wealthy landowners on whose vacant property they had erected shacks.

Once I had been alerted to the organizing theme of the book I could not resist including a section on the role of laughter in a democratic society. Freedom fighters are said to be mirthless people, laughing only at the discomfiture of their enemies. My experience in the struggle had been different. As I had regained consciousness after the operation that saved me from the impact of the car bomb, I told myself a joke. And if humour played a central role in my life and in the freedom struggle, surely it had a key place in an open and democratic society. So, when the question of the lawfulness of parodied appropriation of a trademark arose in the *Laugh it Off* case, I opened my judgment with a query: does the law have a sense of humour?

One of the biggest battles in our constitution-making process had been over whether social and economic rights, such as the right to health, housing, food and education, should be included as fundamental rights in our Bill of Rights. Many of us had fought long and hard to have these 'bread rights' included on a par with 'freedom rights'. Yet once they were so included, the question of how they should be implemented presented serious challenges to the judiciary. How could we give meaningful effect to social and economic rights in a way that, true to the judicial function, did not result in unelected courts usurping the role of the elected government? The pathbreaking case concerned Mrs Grootboom, who found herself homeless, with a thousand other people, sleeping under the stars as the winter rains were approaching. In keeping with the collegial manner in which my Court works, I was able to feed my ideas into the now-famous judgment prepared for the Court by my colleague, Justice Zak Yacoob. In two later cases that dealt with the rights of people living with HIV/AIDS, our Court chamber was packed with people wearing T-shirts reading HIV-POSITIVE. The emotion was palpable, and this time I experienced a reverse osmotic flow—not from life to law, but from law to life. Thus the chapter concludes with a reflection on how objective participation in decisions by the Court impacted on my subjective self, and is entitled 'The Judge Who Cried'.

The *Same-sex Marriages* case was the one that first set me thinking in a very conscious way about the manner in which intense life experiences came to bear on judicial decisions. When preparing a Paul Robeson Lecture for presentation at Columbia University, I became aware of the extent to which two experiences of an apparently contradictory nature had unconsciously driven me to shape my judgment. The first, before I became a judge, involved my showing support for a Gay and Lesbian Pride march. The other was speaking on behalf of the Court at the opening of a conference for Christian Lawyers in Africa. These experiences did not affect the outcome, but they did highlight the importance of dealing with how the secular and the sacred could be reconciled in our new open and democratic constitutional order. A person taking a simplistic view of my past might have predicted a judgment that divided the nation into the enlightened, on the one hand, and the benighted, on the other: the enlightened being those who accepted the emancipatory vision of the Constitution, or at least were tolerant of it, and the benighted those who in bigoted fashion remained trapped in the prejudices of the past. In reality, contact with a diverse range of people in our very heterogeneous society, including both the Pride marchers and the Christian lawyers, had oriented me towards developing what I liked to think was a far more cultivated position. While unequivocally upholding the right of same-sex couples to be treated with the same respect given to heterosexual couples, it would at the same time acknowledge and give constitutional recognition to the depths of conscientious belief held by members of faiths that took a different view.

Finally, the story of the story needed to be told. How do I actually make my decisions and write my judgments (referred to in the United States as opinions)? When teaching a course at the University of Toronto I opened with the words 'Every judgment I write is a lie.' It captured the attention of the students. I explained that the falsehood lay not in the content of the judgment, which I sought to make as honest as possible, but in the discrepancy between the calm and apparently ordered way in which it read, and the intense and troubled jumping backwards and forwards that had actually taken place when it was being written. I felt a need to dispel the notion, induced by the magisterial tone we judges conventionally adopt, that judgments somehow arrive at their destination purely on rational autopilot. This led me to find out that there were four different logics involved in any judgment I wrote: the logic of discovery, the logic of justification, the logic of persuasion, and the logic of preening. And ultimately my thoughts went to the relationship between reason and passion, and then to the concepts of human dignity and proportionality: these interconnected and indivisible concepts run right through the book.

Having grown up in the tradition of the enlightenment I am loath to embrace anything associated with alchemy. But I readily acknowledge that many of the processes that affect our decisions do so in mysterious ways that though not unfathomable in principle, in practice are rather difficult to define. The way life experiences enter into judicial pronouncements, or at least, into my judicial pronouncements, falls into this category. So I simply state that although the alchemy between my oversaturated life and the intense work I do on the Court is strange, it is none the less full of challenge, bafflement and delight. And if the question which emerged from writing this book is 'How do life experiences affect legal decision-making?', the answer is 'In unexpected ways.'

1

Tales of Terrorism and Torture

I was 39 years old, quietly teaching law in exile at Southampton University when I discovered I was a terrorist. I had been invited to attend a conference at Yale University's Contemporary History Department. But I could not get a visa. Why? Because I was a member of the ANC, the African National Congress, led by Nelson Mandela, who had been Commander-in-Chief of Umkhonto We Sizwe (Spear of the Nation) set up to help overthrow apartheid in South Africa. And although I was simply earning my living as a rather innocuous law teacher in England, as a member of the ANC I was a terrorist. Happily, a few months later the political lobby group in Washington which backed the ANC turned out to be stronger than the group hired to promote the interests of the South African government. The State Department policy changed, and I was no longer a terrorist.

It was not simply the ignoble label of 'terrorist' that was so objectionable. In South Africa, being treated as terrorists had brought enormous and terrible consequences for thousands and thousands of us. As terrorists, we could be detained without trial, subject to solitary confinement with no access to family, to lawyers, to anybody. Because? Because the authorities were combating 'terrorism', fighting against what they called the total onslaught against South Africa. And they would bring in the threat of the Soviet Union, and a whole series of perils, the Black peril, the Red peril, and when China became more powerful, the Yellow peril, to justify what they called self-defence against terroristic acts. And we were arbitrarily plucked from our homes and our workplaces and found ourselves in jail.

How difficult it was to be brave! Before it happens, you think that when you are locked up you simply bare your chest, retain belief in your cause, and hold out forever. The reality is totally different. You are living in a little concrete cube. You stare at your toes, you stare at the wall. Your toes, the wall, your toes, the wall, you do not know how long it is going to last. There is nothing to do. There is no one to speak to. It is an inhuman existence. Human beings live in communities, they live with other people. There might be a few individuals who test their spiritual steadfastness by sitting alone on a column for years. I have a friend who is a Buddhist nun; she is silent for a month, for two months. She is in control, it is her choice. Solitary confinement is a non-chosen state, designed not to exalt your spirit through meditation, but to break it down through isolation.

I can still remember how I would try to occupy myself and feel like a valid human being with an active brain and regular emotion. I would try to remember all the states of the United States of America. I think I once got up to 47, but I could not write them down, so after slowly working my way through the alphabet, I would not be sure how many I had counted. I had two arms then, so at least I could get up to 'J'. And then I started singing songs, once more going through the alphabet: *'Always'*, *'Because'*, *'Charmaine'*—quite an interesting profile of the hit tunes of 1963. (I mention in passing that the whole world knew when President Kennedy had been assassinated, except for one person: me. For about a week I had not even an inkling,

I was kept in a world without news, until a security officer could not resist the urge to tell someone who still had not heard.) I would sing, trying to feel like a human being, a person living in the world:

> I'll be living here, always, year after year, always. In this little cell that I know so well. I'll be living swell, always...

and I would be amused that I was using Noel Coward's upper middle class version of an Irving Berlin tune to keep my spirits up:

> I'll be staying in, always, keeping up my chin, always. Not for but an hour, not for but a week, not for 90 days, but always.

I was being held under what was called the 90-day law, which allowed suspects to be locked up in solitary confinement for 90 days without charge. After 90 days of scratching a mark on the wall like a good prisoner, it's the 90th day. I am released, I am given my tie back, my suit is returned—the one that I had worn when I was arrested entering my advocate's chambers—my watch is returned to me, and I say, 'I'm free, I'm free'. And as I am walking out to the street, a sergeant comes up to me—he actually shakes my hand—and says, 'I am placing you under arrest.' And I am on my way back in again, giving up my watch, tie, and suit once more. Ninety days could become another 90 days and another 90 days and another 90 days.

Once you open that door to diminishing respect for the rule of law, you close the door to the rule of law, to *habeas corpus*, to standards of fair interrogation, to the right to a fair trial, the opening or the closing is never enough for the security people. Under pressure to get results, they always want more, and so they ask for 90 days, then 180 days, and eventually for endless detention. That was my first detention, for 90 days and then another 78 days, never knowing when it was going to end.

Two years later (and you don't get stronger each time you are detained), I was detained again and subjected to what I call torture by sleep deprivation. Keeping me up through the day, through the night, with a team of interrogators shouting at me, banging the table for ten minutes, total silence for ten minutes, replacing each other, rotating all the time. When I asked for some food, they seemed delighted, and smirked as they set a plate in front of me: I was pretty sure there was some drug in the food. And the next morning my body is fighting my will, my mind. The desire to sleep, to collapse, is just overwhelming. I knew of people who had held out for four days, for five days or seven days, and the longer they had held out, the more they had ultimately broken. They had lost all control whatsoever. I feared ending up like them. The theory was that you should hold out for 36 hours so that your colleagues could escape. But I had no-one to protect, my information was two years old.

And this battle was not even about information. It was about breaking me. It was about showing that they were stronger, that they were more powerful. I was not thinking of Jean Paul Sartre at the time, but later I recalled his writing about torture in Algeria, and his pointing out that the objective of the relevant sections of the French military was not only to get information, it was to destroy the will, the confidence, the self-esteem of the people in captivity. There was a powerful racist dimension. They sought to de-humanize the people they were torturing by the very act of treating them in a sub-human way. They felt they were not only entitled to do what they were doing, they were obliged to do it because they were combating evil, crushing an inferior, threatening creature. And in the eyes of the interrogators I was in some ways even more terrible than the black people to whom racist ill-treatment had been historically applied. I was the pernicious white mastermind who was stirring up innocent souls, telling them they grievances when in fact they were grateful to this government for making them better off than their counterparts in other parts of Africa.

It was the worst, worst moment of my life. It was not a hypothetical situation of the kind that some academics conjure up when discussing the costs and benefits of the government using torture. And, as in 99.9 per cent recurring of cases where forms of torture are used, there was no ticking bomb nearby when I collapsed on the floor, they poured water on me, and they lifted me up. I still remember those thick, heavy fingers prying my eyes open. I collapsed again, more water, the shoes shuffling around me, some brown, some black and their sense of quiet, methodical urgency, the muted triumph as they were now breaking through my resistance. Any information I had at that stage was stale. Possibly they wanted to get me to be a witness against somebody who had also been in the resistance. That would have been a double triumph, because I could then have been projected as a traitor, as an instrument of the very state I had been opposing. They wanted hegemony, dominance, power, control, mastery. The practice was systematic, it was organized, it was condoned, it was part of policy. And it was integral to the whole system of white supremacy in our country, of retaining an unjust system by using methods which were so ugly and awful that even in apartheid South Africa they were hidden and denied. The rotten apples were at the top of the barrel, not the bottom. Six months, a year or two years later, the torturers would come to court and deny that these things had happened. The judges would look at the witnesses who alleged torture, and would not see blood flowing, or broken bones or burnt skin. They would just see a pale nervous, stuttering accused person claiming abuse, and go on to accept the confident counter-assertions of the security police who, after all, were claiming to protect the judges and their families from terrorist attacks. To their credit, there were judges who showed that even in the direst of situations, space existed for the exercise of independent judicial conscience. But sadly they were few in number.

I remember early on in my first detention thinking to myself that if ever one day I would be in a position of power and authority, I would never do this to another human being. When you are totally powerless, you try to imagine yourself in a situation of command in relation to those who are humiliating you. And what is the greatest power you can exert? It is not to do unto them what they are doing unto you. You are so weak that it is not even feasible, not even imaginable, that you can invert the power relationship. It is more emotionally credible to say to yourself, though I am hurting terribly, I remain superior to them—my standards and values are better than theirs, I have beliefs that are too deep for them to reach, I am a human being, I am fighting for justice, and I am struggling for freedom, I will never be like them. Somehow the strength of that belief, of being able to cling to a vision of a world based on magnanimity rather than on brutal tit-for-tat, gave me a sense of moral triumph that was extremely resilient. Years later when I was writing about the experience of being the target of a car bomb and losing an arm, I found myself repeatedly using the phrase 'and that would be my soft vengeance': if the person accused in a Mozambique Court of being responsible for placing the bomb in my car is put on trial and the evidence is insufficient and he is acquitted—I wrote—that will be my soft vengeance, because we will be living under the rule of law. To gain freedom was a much more powerful vengeance than to impose solitary confinement and torture on the people who had done these things to us. To repay them in kind would have meant that we had become like them, that we had become gangsters and crooks and thugs—for a more noble cause to be sure, but in the end no different from them, only stronger. Our souls would be like their souls, and our inhumanity would be inseperable from their inhumanity.

What made it particularly ironical that we should be punished as terrorists, and in some ways made it especially dreadful, was the fact we were actually strongly against terrorism. In the late 1960s and early 1970s, there were 'isms' all over the place. Capitalism, socialism, imperialism, Stalinism, Trotskyism— only social democracy didn't fit into the 'isms'. And one of the 'isms' that we had denounced on principle in our movement was terrorism. To respond in kind to the violence of apartheid was just wrong. Terrorism was based on the use of indiscriminate violence, directed at civilian people because they happened to belong to a particular group, race, or community. It was totally lacking in political intelligence. It was completely antithetical to our ideals. We were fighting for justice against the system of white supremacy, not against a race. And this lesson was repeated on all our platforms and in all our literature, I would not say *ad nauseam*, but endlessly, as a kind of a mantra of our struggle. For years we believed in the strategy of nonviolence. This was partly to avoid an ultimate racial bloodbath from which we might never recover; you can rebuild destroyed buildings, but it is far more difficult to repair damaged minds seething with hatred passed from generation to generation. So even when every avenue of peaceful protest was proscribed and our movement eventually embarkd on armed resistance, we still denounced any resort to terrorism.

Thus at a time when other movements in the world were conducting spectacular plane high-jacks, and many younger members of the ANC were asking why our leadership were refusing to put our struggle on the map through similar actions, our leadership gave an emphatic 'No.' It was not just that our Acting President, Oliver Tambo, might himself have been travelling on the plane, or somebody else who supported our cause. And it was not simply the danger that our manifestly just struggle against apartheid, against institutionalized racism, would come to be seen merely as a struggle for power and survival between two racial groups. We were preoccupied with the big question: Who was the enemy? The enemy was not a people, a population but a system of injustice. When we used violence in our challenge to that system of injustice, it had always to be directed at the physical power and the structures of domination of that system, not at civilians. And I am convinced that the real reason, the deep reason, that led Oliver Tambo and other leaders of the ANC to repudiate terrorism, was that they did not want us to develop the souls of terrorists. What does terrorism do to those who use it? What kind of person do you become? How could you claim to be a freedom fighter when you kill indiscriminately? I am sure that was the underlying morality, sometimes stated, sometimes implicit. And it was a morality of justice that turned out to be strong, not weak. It constituted a powerful unifying force inside the ANC, enabling it to survive thirty years of exile with no major disputes or breakups, at a time when virtually all other exile movements splintered.

The story moves on to the intense debates we had in the ANC in exile in 1985. Perestroika was barely in its infancy then, so our dilemmas were not related to external international factors. The Berlin Wall was to fall only years later. We had a conference in a small town called Kabwe in Zambia, with Zambian troops surrounding the hall in case South African commandos came to blow us up. It was serious, very, very serious. There were three themes that I remember in particular being discussed. The first was what tactics and strategy we could permissibly use in our struggle. And I recall the speech of King Sabata Dalinyebo, a patriotic traditional leader from the Eastern Cape, who had refused to be a puppet of Pretoria and been forced into exile. I had been host to him and his family in Mozambique, and lent him my bathing costume when we went to the beach—I had never lent bathing trunks to a King before! The theme he was now addressing was how to intensify the struggle to overthrow apartheid. He spoke in isiXhosa, so the small number of us who were culturally backward and could not understand what he was saying (African people had to understand English, the oppressors' language, but the oppressors did not have to understand the languages of the majority) had to wait for the translation. He addressed us in a very animated way, and the audience laughed; and five minutes later when we heard the translation, we also laughed. This was his story: 'Two men are fighting, it's a stick fight, a very bitter one, they are angry and their wives are urging them on. The wife of Man A, shouts: "What's the matter, my husband? You are much stronger than him, and a better fighter, but he's defeating you? You are losing because you only have a stick in one hand, while your other hand is useless for fighting, because it is stupidly holding a blanket to cover your nakedness. Drop the damn blanket, forget your nakedness, and fight with both hands!"' That's when everybody laughed; and when I heard it five minutes later in English, that is when I laughed.

What he was saying was that because of the fear of being labelled terrorist, the ANC was unduly limiting its capacity to hit back. Some delegates were muttering in the corridors that until the whites cried when they buried their children, they would never understand the suffering of the African people. Yet the response of the delegates in the hall was in a very African way to just laugh quietly and gently, as if to say, we get your point, we hear your story, it's a powerful one and we respect you for sharing it with us, but it is not exactly our policy. And the discussion simply moved on. I would have jumped up and said, 'Comrade King (that was how we addressed him), the long-standing policy of the ANC has been to resist terrorism as an ideologically inappropriate instrument of struggle because blah, blah, blah'. The African way was much more subtle, much less confrontational and abrasive. And the result was that Conference fairly and squarely rejected any idea of abandoning the long-standing and principled position of opposition to the use of terrorism.

The second major theme was one which directly involved me. I was then Director of Research in the Ministry of Justice in Mozambique, and Oliver Tambo had invited me to come to speak to him about 'an important matter' in Lusaka, where the ANC had its headquarters. I was curious to know what the 'important matter' was. Eventually I got to his small office. He asked about my health, my family, my work in Mozambique and the political situation there. I remember being amused that one of the great leaders of the age had a rolled-up piece of newspaper, and that he was swatting flies as we conversed. Finally, he came to the point. 'You know, we have a problem in the ANC,' he said, knocking out a fly with a deft flick. 'We've captured a number of people whom we believe were sent by Pretoria to try and destroy the organization. But we don't have any regulations governing how captives should be dealt with. The ANC Constitution deals with annual general meetings, electing new leadership, and so on, and the policy of the organization. But it is silent on the treatment of people we are holding under our control, and we are not sure how to fill that gap.' He paused, despatched another fly, and then added in his polite, lawyerly way, 'I'm sure it's very difficult to get appropriate regulation.' And in my confident way I replied, 'It's not too difficult... the international conventions make it very clear, no torture, inhuman or degrading treatment.' He looked at me and quietly said, 'We use torture.' He spoke with a bleak face. I couldn't believe it. The ANC, an organization fighting for freedom, using torture?

Years later I learnt that people who had been sent by Pretoria to destroy the leadership of the ANC and sabotage its operations, were being held in ANC camps in Angola, and torture had been used against them. It turned out that the ANC leadership had instituted an enquiry and reported that ANC security had indeed used torture, defending themselves by saying that their duty had been to protect the liberation struggle from imminent threats of harm. Now Oliver Tambo was calling me in as a legal person to help the organization establish and apply appropriate standards for dealing with the situation. And in the Oliver Tambo manner, he did not use his position as President of the organization in exile to issue a top-down statement decreeing what the standards should be. He asked me instead to draft a code of conduct which would then be democratically debated by the whole organization at a properly constituted conference.

The problem was to establish the rule of law for a liberation organization in exile, in a context where our host countries expected us to attend to our own legal problems. The document I eventually produced amounted to no less than a code of criminal law and procedure, adapted to the peculiar circumstances of an exiled and dispersed political organization. Of all the legal writings I have done in my life, two stand out as being far more important than any of my books or judgments: the one is the tiny note I smuggled out of jail after I had been tortured by sleep deprivation, and the other this Code of Conduct.

Oliver Tambo was a deeply thoughtful person who believed that the question of whether a liberation organization may use torture to protect itself from serious threats to its fighting capacity, raised profound moral and philosophical questions. He was also a natural democrat who felt that the problem had to be grappled with not just by the leadership but by the whole membership. So the draft was put to all the members in exile (and to some members of the underground in South Africa) to be discussed in advance, so that the branches could take positions on the questions raised. The opinions of the branches were then collated and placed before the delegates at the conference.

I remember the debate vividly. There was overwhelming support for the Code of Conduct as a whole. The delegates were happy with the idea of classifying offences against the organization into three categories, each with its own form of investigation, its own procedures and its own penalties. This presupposed graduated responses to three main categories of people: those who were merely unduly disruptive at branch meetings; those who drove while drunk, or committed offences such as assaults or theft or abuse of women; and those who allegedly had been sent into the organization in order to kill its leaders and wreck its functioning. Tribunals akin to courts were established for the second and third categories, with judicial officers who would be independent, as well as the equivalent of prosecutors and defence counsel, and a right of appeal. It was clear at the conference that the idea of establishing an appropriate system of legality inside the organization strongly appealed to the members.

But there was one issue that called for specific attention, a question that Oliver Tambo felt should not be fudged by the conference. It was whether the Code of Conduct should make special allowance in extremely grave circumstances for what were called 'intensive methods of interrogation'. One by one the young soldiers of Umkhonto We Sizwe came up to the platform and gave their answer: an emphatic no. They declared that the minute you allowed any exceptions or exemptions, elements of ANC security would use them to undermine the principle of not employing torture. They insisted that there be very clear standards and that absolutely no torture be used in any circumstances, whatever the euphemism used. They didn't enter the realms of reasoning of some who speak about where and when to draw the line. Can you torture someone to death because of a ticking bomb? Can you use electrodes or water suffocation, or sleep deprivation? The young soldiers—and the not-so-young lawyers—were making unambiguous statements about the kind of people we were, what we were fighting for, and what our morality and core values were about. They had seen in practice how torture had dehumanized not only the tortured, but the torturers themselves, transforming people who had been their friends, who had left school and university with them to join the freedom struggle, into behaving like brutes. In dealing with brutes, they had allowed themselves to become brutalized, even if only for brief spells. The speakers were adamant. They did not want to belong to an organization that used torture. Full stop.

It was an extraordinary moment for me. Here we were in exile, in perilous conditions facing an extremely powerful, well-organised and quite ruthless enemy. At any moment there could be a commando raid or bombs dropped to take us out. Many of our friends had been tortured to death or assassinated. Yet, I remember a young soldier going to the microphone and saying: 'We are fighting for life—how can we be against life?' He didn't just mean life as creature existence, he meant life as an expression of the human personality, of human dignity. How could we violate the very spirit that kept our rebellion against injustice alive? It was extremely emotional for me to hear this. It corresponded not only to what I knew Oliver Tambo believed in, and what to me was axiomatic, it touched on the core of what had enabled our members to endure the rigours of an extremely harsh struggle and bound us all together.

And it was also absolutely consistent with hard-won principles of international law.

Looking at international law today, I do not see anything that speaks about a ticking bomb justifying evasion of the Torture Convention. Torture is torture, is torture. You go to Argentina, torture is torture. You go to Chile, torture is torture. A generation of people in these countries were subjected to torture;

they know what it is. They have been through it, and they do not convert what is a huge historical experience still haunting the soul of the nation, into a set of imaginary situations to be dealt with at a purely instrumental level, weighing up profits and losses in an analytical book-keeping manner.

I now turn to something often left out of discussions on terrorism, namely, state terrorism. Far more people have been mutilated, exterminated, massacred and killed through state terrorism than through the actions of what are called 'irregular groups'. And in addition to the power that states normally have to kill, maim, torture, and abuse, they also have the capacity to control the media, to terrorize people who otherwise might be witnesses, to impose silence for their deeds and to establish impunity for themselves. I did not take part in the armed struggle. My job was to be a lawyer and a writer and, later an anti-apartheid activist in Europe and in the United States. Yet, the armed struggle came to me. It did so in the form of state terrorism—a bomb placed in my car by South African security agents in Mozambique. I survived. Ruth First didn't survive the letter bomb sent to her at the Centre for African studies at the Eduardo Mondlane University in Maputo. The Maputo cemetery was filled with people assassinated by South African commandos. We were surrounded by death. So when I temporarily regained consciousness in the Maputo Central Hospital, I just felt triumphant. I had survived. This moment, that as a freedom fighter you spent every day wondering about, will it be today, will it be tonight, will it be tomorrow, will I be courageous when it happens to me? It had come, and I had survived, survived, survived. I knew, as a matter of total conviction, that just as I had recovered, my country was going to recover.

And so it came to pass, and eventually the Truth and Reconciliation Commission was set up to deal with the assassinations and tortures of the apartheid era. The Commission was a powerful experience for us in South Africa. So many stories were told, and so many dimensions captured. It wasn't the facts, the data, the information that was important, not even the conclusions. It was seeing the faces, hearing the voices, noting the tears of the victims, and also the crying of the perpetrators as they acknowledged, at least to some degree, their brutal conduct, and now sought amnesty. It was real. These were our people, not strange and depersonalized individuals, 'the enemy', 'the torturers', and 'the security police'. It was Sergeant So-and-so. It was Mrs So-and-so, speaking about her son who had come home with his hair falling out, his poisoned body dying. It was so vivid, a huge national drama in which we were all involved.

One story stood out unforgettably. It symbolized so much. It was the exchange between Tony Yengeni, who had been in the armed wing of the ANC, and Sergeant Benzien, who had tortured him and was now asking for amnesty. We saw on television Tony asking Sergeant Benzien to show the Commission how he had put wet canvas bags over the heads of prisoners. 'Show the Commission how you would smother us until we thought we were drowning, that we would suffocate and die.' The Commission asked someone to lie on the floor, and the bag was put over his head and held there. 'Now please show us how you held it there—how long you held it there.' Sergeant Benzien knelt and kept the bag in place for quite a while. After he stood up, Tony asked him: 'Can you explain how one human being can do this to another human being?' The sergeant started crying. This man who had had power of life and death, who had terrorized others, started crying. His eyes were puffy, his cheeks were red, and tears were streaking down. We saw this one-time state terrorist, under whose hands people might have died, crying, not because he had been physically manhandled but because he had been asked a simple question: How can one person do this to another person?

And somehow that became the dominant theme of the whole Commission: How can people do these things to other people? It was asked with a sense of amazement, of horror. What was at stake was affirmation of the values of our society. It was not just a question of calculating losses and gains, of counterposing the advantages and disadvantages of certain types of state conduct. It was a question of what kind of people we were. What were we about? What kind of country did we live in? Did we have shame, and if so, what were the things that brought it upon us? And the firm corollary of all the testimony and reflection was that it must never happen again. Whoever you are and whatever your motivation, whatever your cause, there are some things human beings just don't do to other human beings. It was that image of the weeping former torturer that became perhaps the most remembered one of the whole truth and reconciliation proceeding.

Sergeant Benzien received his amnesty. He had told the truth. Sending him and the tens of thousands like him to prison, assuming the necessary evidence could have been found, would have achieved very little. But if we got democracy in South Africa, I came to write, then roses and lilies would grow out of my amputated arm. And that would be my soft vengeance. Soft vengeance was powerful. The vow that I had made in solitary confinement was redeeming itself in my life, not as an ideological mechanism to smite others, but as a philosophical and emotional guide pointing to the kind of person I wanted to be, to the kind of country I wanted to live in, and to the sort of Constitution I wished to live under.

The story moves on. I was wearing a green gown and sitting in the Constitutional Court as a judge together with ten other judges, and I was called upon to consider the impact of terrorism on core principles of our new constitutional order. For much of their lives at least half of my colleagues on the Court would have been regarded as terrorists, and the other half as defenders of terrorists. Many of my colleagues had suffered the indignities not only of growing up in severe poverty, but of being subject to humiliating practices simply because they were not white. The present Chief Justice of South Africa once told me wryly as we drove past a building in Durban that as a sixteen year old youth he had been obliged to line up naked there and be hosed down and inspected before being given his 'pass'. He added that as a youngster he could get by, that was life, but what he could not take was seeing men older than his father receiving the same treatment. Another of my colleagues had spent ten years as a prisoner on Robben Island. At least two others, I was sure, had done dangerous work in the underground. Then there were those who, despite having had quite different life experiences that had enabled them to become connoisseurs of good food, wine, and rare books, had as lawyers taken firm and principled stands against apartheid. The Court was very mixed, yet despite our varied life and professional experiences, all of us were totally dedicated to upholding the Constitution. More specifically, all of us were heart and soul in sympathy with the non-racial and non-sexist vision it projected, and totally dedicated to upholding the idea of living in an open and democratic society based on human dignity, equality and freedom.

For my part, I was convinced that if in the 1980s and earlier, we had not taken principled positions on questions of who 'the enemy' was, what methods of struggle were legitimate and how torture was to be prohibited, we would not have achieved what many today regard as the most progressive Constitution in the world. We had in effect created a Bill of Rights at the heart of our struggle, asserting in practical ways our determination to retain our honour and dignity as freedom-fighters, and to re-affirm the principles of justice on which the struggle was founded. It had accordingly not been difficult to move to a constitutional order in a free South Africa based on these very same principles. Our Constitution, then, had deep roots in concepts that had guided us in struggle. It was made by ourselves on our own soil, after patiently following the most inclusive process possible. And its well-honed text, a product of six years of intense negotiations outside and inside Parliament, and finalized after review by our Court according to agreed principles, gave us the instrument to deal with some of the most difficult problems of our era.

One of these problems related to an issue which courts throughout the world were being called upon to address. It was whether persons accused of extremely wicked crimes were entitled to claim the protection of fundamental rights accorded by the very legal order they had apparently set out to destroy. This question lay at the heart of four matters that came to the Constitutional Court.

The first concerned the constitutionality of a provision in the law that established the Truth and Reconciliation Commission. It stated that persons who told the full truth about crimes committed in the course of political conflict, would not only be entitled to amnesty from criminal prosecution but also be protected against claims for civil liability. The immunity from civil claims was challenged as violating the constitutional right to have one's disputes settled in a fair trial. This challenge was a forceful one, but it was rejected by the Court. We held that the Constitution had expressly declared in its epilogue that Parliament could adopt a law that would permit such indemnification. In a particularly eloquent judgment, Ismail Mahomed, Deputy President of the Court and later Chief Justice of South Africa, explained how the achievement of truth and the laying of the foundations for reconciliation, justified the choice that the legislature had made with regard to the best manner of dealing with past atrocities. (See the *AZAPO* case, at p 35, judgment by Mahomed DP.)

The second case concerned Mr Mohamed, who had apparently been involved in the blowing up of the American Embassy in Dar es Salaam. It was a terrible, terrible act, killing about sixty people, some Americans, even more Tanzanians. This was terrorism, pure and simple, not only causing maximum loss of civilian life, but also challenging principles of international law through targeting an international diplomatic institution. After the explosion Mr. Mohamed came down to Cape Town under a false name and registered as a refugee. The FBI tracked him down and without allowing him a lawyer, South African officials handed him over to face capital charges in the USA.

The judgment of our Court was unanimous. It indicated that there was no doubt that Mr Mohamed could lawfully be sent to New York to face trial for the horrendous acts in which he had allegedly participated. But there were two aspects in respect of which the Court felt his rights under the Constitution had been violated. First, there had been no justification for denying him the right to receive legal assistance—the more serious the allegations, the greater the need for a lawyer. Second, and even more important, he should not have been handed over to the American authorities without a guarantee that if found guilty he would not be executed; in our very first case our Court had held unanimously that the death sentence violated the right to dignity and the right not to be subjected to cruel, inhuman or degrading punishment. (See the *Mohamed* case, at p 39, judgment of the Court.)

One could say it was easy enough for judges sitting in Johannesburg, far away from the problems of terrorism, to deliver a beautiful, pure, judgment of little practical import. The fact is, bombs were going off at that time in Cape Town, my home city. We were faced with what can only be described as terrorism. A police investigator and then a magistrate were assassinated by what was said to be a Moslem fundamentalist group. It was a real threat to us. And yet we did not allow the fact that we were living in a very difficult time, with much anxiety and fear around, to influence the decision that we took. There were many voices calling for a return to detention without trial, and yet our country kept its nerve. The killers, the bombers, were caught through good police intelligence, through their ranks being penetrated, through well-prepared prosecutions. The primary breakthrough came because politically their group had become totally isolated, and they had lost their community base. And the more isolated they became, the easier it was to persuade people to give information about their activities, and the more difficult it was for them to find collaborators and safe houses. And now for a decade we have had no activities of that kind, and our Constitution remains intact.

The third case dealt with a trial for conspiracy to commit mass murder. The accused was Dr Wouter Basson, referred to in the newspapers as 'Dr Death'. In the last years of apartheid Dr Basson, a cardiologist of note, had been the head of the South African military's bacteriological and chemical warfare programme. After democracy was achieved, he was put on trial on charges of fraud and conspiracy to murder. The trial judge acquitted him of all the fraud charges, and also quashed the most serious charges against him, namely that he had conspired in South Africa to develop and use poison in Namibia to asphyxiate about 200 members of the South West African People's Organization (SWAPO), who were then taken out in a small plane and dropped into the ocean to drown and be eaten by sharks. The judge stated that it was not possible to try someone in South Africa for conspiracy to commit a crime outside the country's borders.

The matter was widely reported nationally and internationally, and aroused considerable emotion in South Africa. The issue before us at that stage was simply whether the case raised a constitutional matter that could be heard by our Court. Writing separately I emphasized the seriousness of the alleged violations of ancient principles of international humanitarian law, now codified in the Geneva Conventions, and accepted as part of customary international law, which the Constitution called on us to apply. I then set out in detail the manner in which grave crimes against the laws of war were implicated. Having made these points, however, my judgment stressed that the seriousness of the charges should in no way attenuate Dr Basson's right to a fair trial. If anything, I said, the horrendous nature of the charges against him highlighted the importance of a fair trial. It was precisely when alleged crimes threatened basic principles of legality and international law, that the standards associated with the rule of law needed most to be maintained. In this way you do more than just hold an individual to account for breaching the law. You affirm the very principles that the individual is said to have placed under attack. You then defend the rule of law, not by abandoning its principles, but by applying them. (See the *Basson* case, at p 43, separate judgment by myself.)

The fourth case concerned South Africans who had been planning what would have amounted to a terrorist attack elsewhere in Africa. About sixty South Africans, alleged to be mercenaries on their way to stage a bloody coup in Equatorial Guinea, were sitting in jail in Harare, where they had been arrested after their aeroplane had landed to pick up equipment. Their wives, lovers and parents brought an urgent application to our Court asking us to apply the South African Bill of Rights to prevent them from being tortured in Zimbabwe and then being sent on to be tortured and possibly executed after an unfair trial in Equatorial Guinea. The case raised complex and novel questions about the relation between national and international law. But we could not delay our decision for extensive research—what good would a beautifully-prepared judgment have accomplished if it were delivered after the tortures and executions had taken place? So we convened hastily to hear argument during the Court recess. Mercenaries in the past had been responsible for the most heinous crimes in Africa; killers for hire, they were the enemies incarnate of the rule of law. Yet there was something intensely poignant in the way in which the families of the mercenaries sat in hushed groups in the Court chamber, listening respectfully to erudite arguments based on human rights principles that their partners and offspring were said to have despised.

We decided that our government was under an obligation to consider the families' requests seriously, and to do everything within its power, choosing its own timing and methods, to ensure that South African citizens abroad, whatever they might have been planning to do, would not be subjected to unfair trials or to torture. We wrote several judgments, disagreeing on several aspects. But all of us agreed that if gross violations of human rights as protected by international law were threatened, the government was under a legal duty enforceable by the courts to do whatever it could at a diplomatic level to intervene.

At one stage during argument I said to counsel for the applicants, perhaps incautiously, that people who venture into a lion's den should not be surprised if they find a lion there. The press picked up the observation and there was even a cartoon based on it. The exchange with counsel is part of the rough and tumble of legal life, and an important way of getting to legal truth. But in the end, we judges are accountable through the judgments we deliver, and not the questions we ask.

It is difficult to analyse the impact that court decisions have on actual historical events. It may well be that the publicity given to the case, and the evidence and arguments presented had more impact on public life than did the actual decision. Yet any amount of forensic combat, however bitter and prolonged, is better than a single bullet. Submitting the harsh conflicts of our times to legal scrutiny—conducted transparently and in the light of internationally accepted values of fairness and justice— was a telling rebuttal of mercenarism and violence, whether from or against the State. It responded in a practical way to the immediate issues, and at the same time induced governments, judiciaries, and law enforcement agencies in three countries to engage with each other and carefully consider their powers and responsibilities under the international law. It reaffirmed to the South African public that we were living in a constitutional democracy in which all exercises of power were subject to constitutional control. It said something important about the kind of country in which we lived and about the importance of principled and reasoned debate. It underlined that we had moved from a culture of authority and submission to the law, to one of justification and rights under the law.

Anybody sitting on a high court in any land must feel the pressures of the threatening and disturbing events of our times. It would be odd if each one of us were not sensitive to these realities as a judge, as a human being, and as a person. Yet we live in a period when I have felt myself proud not only to be a judge in South Africa, with its exceptional Constitution, but to belong to a world-wide community of judges who believe that basic rights and freedoms matter. The profession of which I am a part was honoured when colleagues in the United States Supreme Court took what I considered to be a principled and carefully-motivated stand on Guantanamo Bay. The same applied when colleagues in the House of Lords Judicial Committee in England took equally principled and well-reasoned positions on torture, and on basic questions of what it meant to live in a free society. If we judges are not here to say through our decisions something profound about what our country stands for when it is being tested, then we are not fulfilling our vocation as judges. And to the extent that I have seen colleagues of mine in other countries with legal structures that do not include the same expansive constitutional provisions that we have, taking positions that keep alive in a meaningful way—not in a demagogic way, but in a meaningful way—the core values of an open and democratic society, then not only do I take pride in our profession, I find burgeoning within myself the hope that at precisely the moments when we are most under stress, we will find the greatest intellectual and moral resources to protect what Lincoln called the 'better angels' of ourselves.

The *Azapo* Case

The issue was whether it was unconstitutional for the law relating to the Truth and Reconciliation Commission to prevent victims of atrocious conduct during the apartheid era from suing perpetrators who had come forward and told the truth to the Commission. South Africa's Truth and Reconciliation Commission has been hailed throughout the world as an example of how a nation can heal itself from the consequences of past atrocities through non-vengeful forms of truth-seeking. It has also been denounced as having provided a morally unacceptable mechanism for allowing perpetrators to avoid being held to account for vicious acts. The Azanian People's Organisation (AZAPO) together with families of victims of atrocities challenged the constitutionality of the statute which not only permitted the Truth and Reconciliation Commission to grant amnesty to torturers and assassins from criminal prosecution but also to free them from civil liability. The Court rejected the challenge holding that the epilogue to the interim Constitution clearly envisaged the granting of comprehensive amnesty to individuals in exchange for revealing the truth of their past misconduct. The following excerpts are from the judgment from Ismail Mahomed, then Deputy President of the Constitutional Court, who later became the first black Chief Justice of South Africa. They deal with agonising choices the drafters of the Constitution had to make.

MAHOMED, DP:

Every decent human being must feel grave discomfort in living with a consequence which might allow the perpetrators of evil acts to walk the streets of this land with impunity, protected in their freedom by an amnesty immune from constitutional attack, but the circumstances in support of this course require carefully to be appreciated. Most of the acts of brutality and torture which have taken place have occurred during an era in which neither the laws which permitted the incarceration of persons or the investigation of crimes, nor the methods and the culture which informed such investigations, were easily open to public investigation, verification and correction. Much of what transpired in this shameful period is shrouded in secrecy and not easily capable of objective demonstration and proof. Loved ones have disappeared sometimes mysteriously and most of them no longer survive to tell their tales. Others have had their freedom invaded, their dignity assaulted or their reputations tarnished by grossly unfair imputations hurled in the fire and the crossfire of a deep and wounding conflict. The wicked and the innocent have often both been victims.

Secrecy and authoritarianism have concealed the truth in little crevices of obscurity in our history. Records are not easily accessible, witnesses are often unknown, dead, unavailable or unwilling. All that often effectively remains is the truth of wounded memories of loved ones sharing instinctive suspicions, deep and traumatising to the survivors but otherwise incapable of translating themselves into objective and corroborative evidence which could survive the rigours of the law. The Truth and Reconciliation Act seeks to address this massive problem by encouraging these survivors and the dependents of the tortured and the wounded, the maimed and the dead to unburden their grief publicly, to receive the collective recognition of a new nation that they were wronged, and crucially, to help them to discover what did in truth happen to their loved ones, where and under what circumstances it did happen and who was responsible. That truth, which the victims of repression seek so desperately to know, is in the circumstances, much more likely to be forthcoming if those responsible for such monstrous misdeeds are encouraged to disclose the whole truth with the incentive that they will not receive the punishment which they undoubtedly deserve if they do.

Without that incentive there is nothing to encourage such persons to make the disclosures and to reveal the truth which persons in the position of the applicants so desperately desire. With that incentive, what might unfold are objectives fundamental to the ethos of a new constitutional order. The families of those unlawfully tortured, maimed or traumatised become more empowered to discover the truth, the perpetrators become exposed to opportunities to obtain relief from the burden of a guilt or an anxiety they might be living with for many long years, the country begins the long and necessary process of healing the wounds of the past, transforming anger and grief and structured climate essential for the 'reconciliation and reconstruction' which informs the very difficult and sometimes painful objective of the amnesty articulated in the epilogue.

The alternative to the grant of immunity from criminal prosecution of offenders is to keep intact the abstract right to such a prosecution for particular persons without the evidence to sustain the prosecution successfully, to continue to keep the dependants of such victims in many cases substantially ignorant about what precisely happened to their loved ones, to leave their yearning for the truth effectively unassuaged, to perpetuate their legitimate sense of resentment and grief and correspondingly to allow the culprits of such deeds to remain perhaps physically free but inhibited in their capacity to become active, full and creative members of the new order by a menacing combination of confused fear, guilt, uncertainty and sometimes even trepidation.

The amnesty contemplated is not a blanket amnesty against criminal prosecution for all and sundry, granted automatically as a uniform act of compulsory statutory amnesia. It is specifically authorised for the purposes of effecting a constructive transition towards a democratic order. It is available only where there is a full disclosure of all facts to the Amnesty Committee and where it is clear that the particular transgression was perpetrated during the prescribed period and with a political objective committed in the course of the conflicts of the past.

The election made by the makers of the Constitution was to permit Parliament to favour 'the reconstruction of society' involving in the process a wider concept of 'reparation', which would allow the state to take into account the competing claims on its resources but, at the same time, to have regard to the 'untold suffering' of individuals and families whose fundamental human rights had been invaded during the conflict of the past.

The choice of alternatives legitimately fell within the judgment of the lawmakers. The exercise of that choice does not, in my view, impact on its constitutionality.

The *Mohamed* Case

The issue was the lawfulness of the deportation to the United States of a person to face charges of terrorism without first obtaining an assurance that if found guilty he would not be executed.

The judgment was delivered in the name of the Court.

THE COURT:

Mohamed entered South Africa under an assumed name using a false passport. He applied for asylum giving false information in support of his application and was issued with a temporary visa to enable him to remain in South Africa while his application was being considered. Those facts justified the South African government in deporting him. That, however, is only part of the story, for the crucial events are those that happened after Mohamed had secured his temporary visa. Having been identified by the FBI as a suspect for whom an international arrest warrant had been issued in connection with the bombing of the United States embassy in Tanzania, he was apprehended by the South African immigration authorities in a joint operation undertaken in cooperation with the FBI. Within two days of his arrest and contrary to the provisions of the Act he was handed over to the FBI by the South African authorities for the purpose of being taken to the United States to be put on trial there for the bombing of the embassy. On his arrival in the United States he was immediately charged with various offences relating to that bombing and was informed by the court that the death sentence could be imposed on him if he were convicted. That this was likely to happen must have been apparent to the South African authorities as well as to the FBI when the arrangements were made for Mohamed to be removed from South Africa to the United States.

Another suspect, Mr. Mahmoud Mahmud Salim, alleged to be a party to the conspiracy to bomb the embassies, was extradited from Germany to the United States. Germany has abolished capital punishment and is also party to the European Convention on Human Rights. The German government sought and secured an assurance from the United States government as a condition of the extradition that if he is convicted, Salim will not be sentenced to death. This is consistent with the practice followed by countries that have abolished the death penalty.

By committing ourselves to a society founded on the recognition of human rights we are required to give particular value to the rights of life and dignity, and that 'this must be demonstrated by the State in everything that it does'. In handing Mohamed over to the United States without securing an assurance that he would not be sentenced to death, the immigration authorities failed to give any value to Mohamed's right to life, his right to have his human dignity respected and protected and his right not to be subjected to cruel, inhuman or degrading punishment.

[*The Court underlined the positive obligation that the Bill of Rights imposed on the State to 'protect promote and fulfil the rights in the Bill of Rights'. It then proceeded to hold that:*] [f]or the South African government to cooperate with a foreign government to secure the removal of a fugitive from South Africa to a country of which the fugitive is not a national and with which he has no connection other than that he is to be put on trial for his life there, is contrary to the underlying values of our Constitution. It is inconsistent with the government's obligation to protect the right to life of everyone in South Africa, and it ignores the commitment implicit in the Constitution that South Africa will not be party to the imposition of cruel, inhuman or degrading punishment...

The handing over of Mohamed to the United States government agents for removal by them to the United States was unlawful. That is a serious finding. South Africa is a young democracy still finding its way to full compliance with the values and ideals enshrined in the Constitution. It is therefore important that the State lead by example. This principle cannot be put better than in the celebrated words of Justice Brandeis in Olmstead et al v United States: 'In a government of laws, existence of the government will be imperilled if it fails to observe the law scrupulously... Government is the potent, omnipresent teacher. For good or for ill, it teaches the whole people by its example... If the Government becomes a law-breaker, it breeds contempt for the law; it invites every man to become a law unto himself; it invites anarchy.' The warning was given in a distant era but remains as cogent as ever. Indeed, for us in this country, it has a particular relevance: we saw in the past what happens when the State bends the law to its own ends and now, in the new era of constitutionality, we may be tempted to use questionable measures in the war against crime. The lesson becomes particularly important when dealing with those who aim to destroy the system of government through law by means of organised violence. The legitimacy of the constitutional order is undermined rather than reinforced when the State acts unlawfully. Here South African government agents acted inconsistently with the Constitution in handing over Mohamed without an assurance that he would not be executed and in relying on consent obtained from a person who was not fully aware of his rights and was moreover deprived of the benefit of legal advice.

The *Basson* Case

The issue was whether a constitutional matter was raised by the decision of a trial court to quash charges of conspiracy to murder against the former head of South Africa's bacteriological and chemical warfare programme. I wrote a separate judgment supporting the view of my colleagues that a constitutional question was indeed raised, entitling our Court to hear the matter.

SACHS J:

The questions before us have to be determined in the complex historical and jurisprudential situation in which the South African state had moved from perpetrating grave breaches of international humanitarian law to providing constitutional protection against them. Issues which in another context might appear to be purely technical concerning the interpretation of a statute or the powers of a court on appeal, took on profoundly constitutional dimensions in the context of war crimes.

Nothing shows greater disrespect for the principles of equality, human dignity and freedom than the clandestine use of State power to murder and dispose of opponents. It follows that any exercise of judicial power which has the effect of directly inhibiting the capacity of the State subsequently to secure accountability for such conduct goes to the heart of South Africa's new constitutional order. When the depredations complained of are of such a dimension as to transgress the frontier between ordinary State-inspired criminal violence and war crimes, the engagement with the core of the Constitution becomes even more intense.

It is in this context that the interim constitution provided for the establishment of the Truth and Reconciliation Commission (the TRC). Its objective was to build a bridge between the past and the present and enable an appropriate balance between all the public and private interests involved. The respondent has not chosen to have recourse to the TRC process. We are accordingly left to deal with the matter on the basis of applying the ordinary principles of law and statutory interpretation as viewed and developed in the light of the Constitution. In the present case I believe the consequences of the decision of the trial court to quash the charges and the subsequent refusal of the Supreme Court of Appeal to entertain an appeal against the decision, do impact directly on the legal order as envisaged by the Constitution, particularly insofar as war crimes may be involved. They touch on the central features of our constitutional democracy. As such they are determinative of the issue before us at this stage, namely whether the questions raised in the application for leave to appeal, are constitutional matters.

It should be emphasized that none of the above should be taken as suggesting that because war crimes might be involved the rights to a fair trial of the respondent as constitutionally protected are in any way attenuated. When allegations of such serious nature are at issue, and where the exemplary value of constitutionalism as against lawlessness is the very issue at stake, it is particularly important that the judicial and prosecutorial functions be undertaken with rigorous and principled respect for basic constitutional rights. The effective prosecution of war crimes and the rights of the accused to a fair trial are not antagonistic concepts. On the contrary, both stem from the same constitutional and humanitarian foundation, namely the need to uphold the rule of law and the basic principles of human dignity, equality and freedom.

The *Kaunda* Case

The issue was whether the South African government was under a legal duty to give what protection it could to South African mercenaries captured in Zimbabwe and faced with possibilities of torture and execution in Equatorial Guinea. In a separate judgment I supported colleagues who held emphatically that such a duty existed. I pointed out that the South African Constitution made it clear that one of the principles governing national security was that 'the resolve to live in peace and harmony precludes any South African citizen from participating in armed conflict, nationally or internationally except as provided for in terms of the Constitution or national legislation.'

SACHS J:

Mercenary activities aimed at producing regime-change through military coups violated this principle in a most profound way. The government is under a duty to act resolutely to combat them, the more so if they are hatched on South African soil.

At the same time, [the Constitution] provides that: 'The security services must act, and must teach and require their members to act, in accordance with the Constitution and the law, including customary international law and international agreements binding on the Republic.' This section emphasises that in dealing with even the most serious threats to the state, a noble end does not justify use of base means. . . .

The values of our Constitution and the human rights principles enshrined in international law are mutually reinforcing, interrelated and, where they overlap, indivisible. South Africa owes much of its very existence to the rejection of apartheid by the organized international community and the latter's concern for the upholding of fundamental human rights. It would be a strange interpretation of our Constitution that suggested that adherence by the government in any of its activities to the foundational norms that paved the way to its creation was merely an option and not a duty.

In my opinion, the government has a clear and unambiguous duty to do whatever is reasonably within its power to prevent South Africans abroad, however grave their alleged offences, from being subjected to torture, grossly unfair trials and capital punishment. At the same time, the government must have an extremely wide discretion as to how best to provide what diplomatic protection it can offer.

[*We later learned through the media that the applicants had been sentenced under Zimbabwean law to terms of imprisonment of about one year each, with their leader receiving seven years, while most of the accused later put on trial in Equatorial Guinea were found guilty of plotting a coup, and despite the prosecution asking for the death sentence, imposed only sentences of imprisonment, the highest being for thirty-four years.*]

2

Tock-Tick: The Working of
a Judicial Mind

'Every judgment I write is a lie.' This was the opening sentence of a lecture I gave some years back to students at the University of Toronto. It disturbed the somnambulistic certainty that many of them possessed. Legal judgments, I sought to tell them, did not emerge from the dispassionate placing of logical propositions in rationally ordained sequence. Now, I can perhaps soften the statement a little: every judgment I write tells a lie against itself.

As a new judge on the Constitutional Court I would always smile inwardly when first reading the printed version of a judgment of mine. It told its story in such an orderly, clear, sequential narrative form. The opening would state the issues raised. It would then set out the history of the litigation and elucidate the specific questions to be determined. Next it would outline the relevant legal principles involved, apply them to the facts of the case and arrive at an appropriate conclusion. There would be a simple forward progression—tick-tock—the tick always coming before the tock. Yet in reality the tock had often long preceded the tick. Indeed, it was not unusual for the very last sentence I wrote to be the opening statement declaring what the case would be all about.

My judgments in fact emerge from an inchoate—even chaotic—mental firmament quite different from that suggested by their ultimate assured expression. Mixed in with the formal logic there has invariably been an enormous amount of random intuitive searching and a surging element of unruly, free-floating sensibility. At times I almost feel a sense of indignation that the apparently serene, relatively bland and cool document is all that remains of the actual warm and agitated process involved in its production.

My experience suggests that legal writing is not simply or even primarily about connecting pure, rational legal propositions together to produce a forward-moving train of thought that arrives at a logically pre-destined terminus. Though internal rationality is necessary, it is only one part of the story. The actual journey of a judgment starts with the most tentative exploratory ideas, and passes through large swathes of doubt and contestation before finally ending up as a confident exposition purportedly excluding any possibility of error. The erratic, even contradictory pathways, are hidden. I have been surprised by how intricate and difficult judgment-writing in fact is.

I do not advance these propositions as a legal analyst taking part in jurisprudential debate. Rather, I present them as a participant/observer of processes I actually live through. The first engagement with a case comes when I read the papers lodged by the parties with the Court. Certain intuitive responses develop and tentative thoughts emerge about how the case might go. My clerks then prepare a memo, which we discuss in a very open-ended way. At that stage, the main task is to delineate the legal issues involved. Then, on the eve of the oral hearing in court, I re-read the papers, and jot down some key questions to be put to counsel. At the actual hearing certain themes, ideas and possible forms of resolution start presenting themselves with a degree of urgency. But I rein in any tendency to arrive at a firm conclusion. I certainly do not commit myself at that stage to a fixed process of hard, formal reasoning. An important feature of our Court is that to prevent ourselves from being unduly influenced by the views of colleagues, we do not discuss cases before the hearing is held. The result is a constant fascination with the questions put by my colleagues to counsel: could there be so many possible ways of looking at the matter that I have not even thought of? And frequently, to adapt Milton, any confusion I already have is worse confounded.

The fact that my initial responses to legal issues are intuitive rather than strongly reasoned is not cause for alarm. By the time one is appointed to sit on a Court like ours, one's intuitions are not based on blind, untutored and highly subjective predilections. Nor can they be seen simply as the residue of books read, or, in my case, of years of political activism, or life in prison or in exile, or as a victim of a bomb attack. These life experiences have certainly played a profound role in shaping my world view. But as far as my legal thinking is concerned, they have been filtered and transmuted into an evolving lexicon of legal principles which I share with others who have followed quite different journeys.

To say that every judgment I write tells a lie against itself should not be understood as in any way softening the need to abominate lying in public life. Just as nature abhors a vacuum, so a constitutional state repudiates lying, totally. Openness and integrity are not merely the virtues of honest individuals, they are the core elements of the trust that should bind citizens and government together in a single polity. And the institution which, above all, should tell no lies or be false in any way, is the Judiciary. To those who would trivialize the judicial process, representing it as a flabby subjective response dressed up in the false guise of objectivity, I offer the following: while one should always be sceptical about the law's pretensions, one should never be cynical about the law's possibilities.

I can only speak about judgments that I myself have written. It is quite possible that my colleagues sit down and directly, without pause, reason their way logically through the sequence that finally appears in their judgments. Yet I have my doubts. My Court by its nature deals only with borderline cases. Ours is basically a court of appeal that controls its docket and excludes hopeless matters. If we only enrol appeals that have a reasonable prospect of success, they might or might not succeed. They are never hopeless. By definition the matters we hear resist straightforward solution, and the members of the Court can quite honestly go this way or that. And frequently we find ourselves torn; one of my colleagues is fond of saying that he 'excruciated' before coming to a decision. Indeed it is difficult to imagine a judgment on a complex issue simply writing itself.

And we are not a Court for the complacent. There are eleven of us, and our quorum is eight. We perpetually stir in new ideas, different approaches. And elements of undue personal subjectivity vaporize quickly in the cauldron of argument. It matters very much to enjoy the good opinion of our colleagues. We are aware that we are simultaneously both heirs to a timeless international tradition, and promoters of a new constitutional jurisprudence, this in a country that both longs for transformation and desperately needs predictability. We meet round the conference table once, twice, three times and more, seated where we wish, and engage with each other in the intense and distinctly earnest deliberative tones that only jurists (and some clerics) use. You

can almost hear our brains whirring as one by one we motiv-
ate our different standpoints. After the meetings, we send each
other courteous but sharp e-mails. In a setting of rigorous intellectual interchange, any initial naked preferences that we might
have started with will at least have to be artfully dressed up in
the garb of plausible legal argument.

To say that every judgment I write tells a lie against itself,
should not, then, be seen as stating that every statement I make
has to be disbelieved (which would get me into a logical bind,
because the very statement itself would have to be disbelieved).
It is limited to pointing out that an enormous incongruity exists
between the surface character of my judgments as they appear
in the law reports or on the internet, and the actual intellectual
programme in terms of which they have been devised, created,
constructed, and formalized. This, then, is the falsity: the pre-
tence implicit in the presentation of a judgment that it has been
written exactly in the way it appears. All hesitations, sometimes
even reversals of position on certain points, have been eviscer-
ated from the final version. All to-ing and fro-ing in the process
of its construction has been eliminated. Completely left out of
account is the complexity of the process by which the final reasoned decision has been arrived at. In sum, the final format of
the judgment belies the manner in which it has been produced.

As it turned out, it fell to some political science professors
from the University of Toronto to resolve the apparent contradictions that puzzled me. The University had a practice of
arranging for visiting professors to be taken out to dinner to
a different restaurant each night. I had first thought this was
to spare us from dining alone in our hotels, only to discover
that there was no free dinner: each meal was in fact a seminar.

And it turned out that the political science professors were not at all disconcerted when I told them why I thought that every judgment of mine was a lie. 'Oh,' they replied, 'we know about that...it's the difference between the logic of discovery and the logic of justification.' They explained that any scientist was familiar with the difference, as if to say they were not surprised that lawyers did not know about it. Whether working in natural science or in political science, people had long realized that discovery was a specific process with its own logic, its own pre-conditions and, by its nature, its own surprises. The logic of justification, on the other hand, was based on the conjunction of verifiable evidence and logical reasoning to produce replicable results. The outcome had to be what the outcome was. Whereas justification depended on the affirmation of certainty, discovery was based on rendering uncertain what had previously been regarded as sure.

In mature supreme courts, legal debate tends to revolve not around the enunciation of new principles, but around expanding or contracting the outer frontiers of the court's own precedent. Only rarely are there moments of great judicial advance when completely new principles are established. In our case, however, being a new court with a new constitution, and, moreover, a court that is encouraged to look to international jurisprudence, the enunciation of innovatory principles has been our staple. Our primary challenge has been to lay secure foundations for a transformative constitutional jurisprudence. Yet for all the differences between the work of our new Court and that of, say, the mature United States Supreme Court, my sense is that we simply write large what are universal processes of evolving judicial reasoning, wherever and whatever the court.

Acknowledging that there are separate processes of discovery and justification has undoubtedly helped me to understand why my experience of judgment-writing has been turbulent. It has not, however, left me at large to choose arbitrarily between discovery (intuition) and justification (logic). Justification means using certain accepted principles, rules, and standards to arrive at a conclusion that is consistent with those rules, principles, and standards. A discovery that cannot be justified simply cannot stand. Indeed justification is based on obligation, on the rationale being underpinned by logical necessity. Accordingly, one does not have a free choice between adopting one's intuitive sense—that intense feeling emerging inside yourself based on a lifetime of experience—and following the process of formal reasoning.

The dictates of formal reasoning will at times cause me to abandon even the strongest initial intuitions, putting my judicial nose quite out of joint. Thus in a case that dealt with whether the criminal prohibition of prostitution and brothel-keeping violated constitutional rights to freedom and privacy, my firm inclination had been that the state had a right to regulate the furnishing of sex for reward, but not to criminalize it. My strong belief was that to use the criminal law to attempt to suppress prostitution was not only ineffective, but hypocritical. As Sir Sydney Kentridge, renowned advocate from Johannesburg and barrister in London, had once told me, the Maida Vale street in which he now lived had in the puritanical nineteenth century been famous for the love parlours to which members of the British parliament had driven in their carriages after their day's work. Yet the Constitution required us when interpreting the Bill of Rights to promote the values of an open and democratic society based on human dignity, equality, and freedom. This led me to do an extensive search into the way in which the law in a large number of open and democratic societies treated prostitution. To my total dismay, the research established that whatever the practice on the ground might have been, very few democratic societies officially adopted an approach similar to the one I intuitively felt to be correct. I was accordingly compelled to re-cast my thinking and dutifully accept a result I found to be most disconcerting. All I could do was to indicate that when Parliament came to consider the matter, one of its options would be to follow the process of decriminalization. Though conceptually messy, neither giving legal recognition to paid sex work, nor applying criminal penalties to it, de-criminalization would accurately reflect societal ambivalence and diminish the problems of law enforcement. The humbling consequences of my legal research are reflected in the *Jordan* case (see p 59).

It is precisely the interplay between the different orders of discovery and logic that makes our life on the bench so exacting (and so intellectually exciting). As we wrestle with a problem, we go to-and-fro, backwards and forwards, from logic to discovery, from discovery to logic. The tocks and the ticks are in great disharmony, until eventually we feel we have settled the tension, and what might have been tock-tick, tick-tick-tick, tock-tock, at last become tick-tock, tick-tock, tick-tock. So, unlike a clock which has progressed from six o'clock to twelve o'clock in a graduated way, inexorably impelled by the logic impressed into its mechanism, we jump backwards and forwards according to the vagaries of our thinking and the fits and starts of our writing processes.

It is the invariably erratic nature of the process of my judgment-writing that explains why the very last words that I often insert into my judgment are to be found right at the beginning: 'This case raises questions about...' I write this opening sentence only after having looked at what has emerged as the extended text of the judgment, at a time when I am able to get a full overview of the argument and discern the key threads that hold it together. Indeed, I sometimes discover at a fairly late stage a determinative logic lying beneath the meandering passages that clamours for explicit acknowledgment. It is almost, as sculptors would have it, that the story is in the marble, or in the wood. Then, and only after having disinterred the connecting logic and tightened up the presentation, do I feel confident enough to finalize the opening sentence. And, I should mention, this declaration of what is the fundamental issue—the problematic to be resolved—often turns out to be quite different from that which I had confidently asserted in my first draft.

Learning about the logic of discovery and the logic of justification went a long way towards helping me understand the convoluted processes I engaged in when writing a judgment. And yet I felt there was something more to what I was doing than just achieving harmony between discovery and justification. A third element had to be included—the logic of persuasion.

Persuasion depends on justification. If there is a gap in the process of reasoning, the judgment will be manifestly flawed and nobody will be persuaded. But persuasion involves far more than rational exposition. If the word 'rhetoric' did not have such a negative connotation in the English language, I would liken persuasion to the rhetorical thrust of a judgment. Rhetoric is the kind of argumentation that convinces, that connects up the specific issues of the case with the wider realms of human experience. In particular it taps into the powerful mystique built up by the law over the ages. Law lives not by reason alone. Mystique is central to the legal imagination. Though concepts like the rule of law and judicial independence are all underpinned by technical legal rules, they cannot be understood simply as the aggregate of these rules. They have a global resonance and appeal that has spanned centuries and transcended continents. Rhetoric succeeds, then, when it establishes compelling links between what Cardozo aptly referred to as the sordid facts of a particular case and the shining legal truths of the ages.

It might be that some judges are so well-focused and intellectually confident that they can sum up what they want to say in one powerful statement, without even taking a breath. But most of us cannot. Perhaps we do not even *want* to be so spartan. We feel the need to explore the wider dimensions of the issue, to understand the context, to appreciate the impact of our reasoning on those affected by it, and generally to handle the problems in ways that penetrate resonantly into widely shared legal imagining. We want to bring other people on board, and we know that it is often the image, the parallel example, the spelling out of the implications, that convinces. In short, it is the legal rhetoric that persuades, and not just the formal logic that underpins it.

Finally, I would add a fourth ingredient as part of the judgment-writing mix. It is what I call preening. Preening is that little bit of show-off that adds a distinctive voice and register to the exposition. If you like it, you call it the 'sparkle'; if you don't, you refer to it as the 'gas'. When I am reading judgments from other jurisdictions, there are certain ringing pronouncements that just reach out to me. They make me feel proud to be a lawyer, to be involved in the judicial enterprise. As I have said, the law depends heavily on mystique. The very notion of justice has a profound moral-historical dimension. Concepts such as the rule of law, fundamental rights and the independence of the judiciary, occupy distinctive, hallowed spaces from which powerfully attractive energies radiate. If appropriately used, these principles can provide a sense of shape, of dignity, of style, of historical timbre to judicial argument. And again, provided it is kept under control, I do not feel that a little bit of preening, or to put it more kindly, some carefully modulated expression of judicial pride, is out of keeping with the restraint expected of a judge.

It would, of course, be reprehensible to go in for headline-seeking. The temptations of judicial populism, which offer shallow judicial sound bites without any real jurisprudential content, are great. In our country judges do not run for office, nor, I like to think, do we crave name recognition. But I do not feel there is anything wrong in employing a resounding phrase or sharp image that is potentially memorable, even if the judgment could survive very well, and some might say even better, without it. The fact is that few activities are more in the public domain than adjudicating on the lives of our fellow human beings, and few have more public significance than exerting control over the government that pays our salary. We should accordingly not see it as a virtue for the public to regard us as anonymous, faceless ciphers. We should take responsibility for our own decisions, and not be fearful to speak in our own voices.

What do all the above ruminations signify the next time a judgment starts with the name 'SACHS J'? However joyfully the text might seek to proclaim the good legal news, its birth will have been totally un-immaculate. The more elegant and compact it is, the more persuasive and easy to read, the more will it have had to survive multiple excruciating labours. And the more intensely collegial the court, the more will my unconscious predilections prompted by personal life experiences have been mediated by the views of fellow judges. Working in multi-member courts with systems of appeals may not automatically eviscerate and neutralize the subjective experiences of each judge, but it does provide for a rich mix of individual consciences. Listening not only to the formal logic of my colleagues but attuning myself to their inner registers, produces major changes to my drafts. None of these, however, are acknowledged in the version as finally delivered. The published judgment excludes huge amendments, additions, and excisions, and includes large chunks taken from comments made by colleagues. And it neither discloses which passages were introduced precisely to meet criticisms by colleagues, nor identifies those paragraphs that were taken from pieces of paper with epiphanous discoveries spontaneously scrawled upon them.

Simple, clear, persuasive to the legal community—that is my dream. And to the extent that I realize that dream, the judgment misleads the reader as to its provenance. The paradox is that to achieve that misrepresentation, I invest all my honesty, I labour and labour again, think and re-think, test and re-test the logic, and examine and re-examine the arguments presented for and against by my colleagues. And the end result is that the greater and more successful the honesty of the endeavour, the greater the falsehood of the presentation. Tock-Tick.

POSTSCRIPT: If anyone suggests that this Chapter tells a lie against itself, I neither confirm nor deny.

The *Jordan* Case

In this matter the Court dealt with the constitutionality of a law that penalised the offering of sex for reward. The Court divided 6 to 5. We could not even agree on whether to call it prostitution or sex-work. Our differences, however, were not primarily over terminology or even policy—I suspect that most if not all of us would have preferred regulation to criminalization. Our main divergence was on whether the question was intrinsically one of policy to be determined by the legislature the majority position, or raised an issue of fundamental constitutional rights to be decided by the courts, as contended for in the minority judgment co-authored by myself and Justice Kate O'Regan. A feature of the evidence had been the way feminists had divided: some had asserted that the law was necessary to denounce prostitution as the ultimate form of female subordination, others had insisted that it was the law that led to oppression of women by making sex workers vulnerable to violence, crime and ill-health. We come to the conclusion, reluctantly, on my part, that this was an issue on which open and democratic societies differ. Nevertheless, in our view the statute discriminated unfairly against women by identifying as candidates for prosecution females rather than males.

O'REGAN AND SACHS JJ:

The Court cannot decide, on the papers for example, whether criminalisation is necessary to reduce an activity that is conducive to violence, or whether it is the criminalisation itself that establishes conditions for violence. Without doubt, the relationship between cause and effect in all these matters is complex. These are contested issues throughout the globe. Moreover, they are matters upon which Legislatures in open and democratic societies may legitimately and reasonably disagree as to the most appropriate legal response in their own society.

In approaching the question of proportionality concerning the degree to which the right to privacy is limited, the Court is obliged to apply the standards of an open and democratic society. Open and democratic societies vary enormously in the manner in which they characterise and respond to prostitution. Thus practice in such countries ranges from allowing prostitution but not brothel-keeping; to allowing both; suppressing both; to setting aside zones for prostitution; and to licensing brothels and collecting taxes from them. The issue is generally treated as one of governmental policy expressed through legislation rather than one of constitutional law to be determined by the courts. We are unaware of any successful constitutional challenge in domestic courts to laws prohibiting commercial sex. The matter appears to have been treated as one for legislative choice and not one for judicial determination. The issue is an inherently tangled one where autonomy, gender, commerce, social culture and law enforcement capacity intersect. A multitude of differing responses and accommodations exist, and public opinion is fragmented and the women's movement divided. In short, it is precisely the kind of issue that is invariably left to be resolved by the democratically accountable law-making bodies.

We, therefore, conclude that, although nearly all open and democratic societies condemn commercialised sex, they differ vastly in the way in which they regulate it. These are matters appropriately left to deliberation by the democratically elected bodies of each country. Voices such as those of the Gender

Commission, SWEAT [Sex Worker Education and Advocacy Taskforce] and the RHRU [Reproductive Health and Research Unit] will help direct public and parliamentary attention to the constitutional goal of the achievement of equality between men and women.

[Justice O'Regan and I went on to express our disagreement with the majority on whether the law discriminated unfairly on the ground of gender. Our view was that it did do so because it applied double standards to females who offered sex for reward, and males who paid for it. We acknowledged that on its face, the law was gender neutral, and that theoretically the 'johns' could be prosecuted as co-conspirators to the offence. Nevertheless our joint judgment went on as follows:]

In imposing a direct criminal liability for the prostitute, the law chooses to censure and castigate the conduct of the prostitute directly. The indirect criminal liability on the client, assuming there is such, flows only from the crime committed by the prostitute who remains the primary offender. The primary crime and the primary stigma lie in offering sexual intercourse for reward, not in purchasing it.

This distinction is, indeed, one which for years has been espoused both as a matter of law and social practice. The female prostitute has been the social outcast, the male patron has been accepted or ignored. She is visible and denounced, her existence tainted by her activity. He is faceless, a mere ingredient in her offence rather than a criminal in his own right, who returns to respectability after the encounter. In terms of the sexual double standards prevalent in our society, he has often been regarded either as having given in to temptation, or as having done the sort of thing that men do. Thus, a man visiting a prostitute is not considered by many to have acted in a morally reprehensible fashion. A woman who is a prostitute is considered by most to be beyond the pale.

The inference is that the primary cause of the problem is not the man who creates the demand but the woman who responds to it: she is fallen, he is at best virile, at worst weak. Such discrimination, therefore, has the potential to impair the fundamental human dignity and personhood of women.

The salient feature of the differentiation in the present matter is that it tracks and reinforces in a profound way double standards regarding the expression of male and female sexuality. The differential impact is accordingly not accidental, just as the failure of the authorities to prosecute male customers as accomplices is entirely unsurprising. They both stem from the same defect in our justice system which would hold women to one standard of conduct and men to another.

We see no reason why the plier of sex for money should be treated as more blameworthy than the client. If anything, the fact that the male customers will generally come from a class that is more economically powerful might suggest the reverse. Parliament may decide to render criminal sexual intercourse where a reward is paid, but their decision to make only purveyors of sexual intercourse and not purchasers primarily liable, entrenches the deep patterns of gender inequality which exist in our society and which our Constitution is committed to eradicating.

3

A Man Called Henri: Truth, Reconciliation, and Justice

An Encounter

I was in my chambers when I received a message from reception that somebody calling himself 'Henri' had arrived to see me. I went to the security entrance with a measure of anticipation. Henri had telephoned a few days earlier to say that he was going to testify to the Truth and Reconciliation Commission about the bomb which had exploded in my car and caused the loss of my right arm. Naturally I was keen to see the person who had the courage, or the foolhardiness, or just the interest, to want to see me.

I opened the door with my security pass and a slender, youngish man came forward. He introduced himself as Henri and gave his surname. He had been, I think, a Captain in the South African Defence Force, and he strode down the passage to my chambers with not quite a swagger, but a military gait, and I strolled along at his side with what I supposed to be a jaunty judicial ambulation.

We sat down and started talking. I am sure he was as puzzled about me as I was about him. He explained quickly that his role had simply been to take the photographs and prepare a dossier for the persons who were ultimately to place the bomb in my car. He said that he had in fact dropped out of the operational group some months before the explosion, so he could not give any testimony directly as to what had happened. But he knew the group that was involved, he knew the structure, and he was going to go to the Truth and Reconciliation Commission to tell his story and ask for amnesty for his part.

I was not quite sure why he had come to tell me this. I wanted to know more about him. Who was this person, whom I had never seen until that moment, who did not know me, who had no anger towards me, whom I did not hate, for whom I was just a figure-head, and who had tried to extinguish my life? What had passed through his head, how had he functioned, and how did he fit into the group that was on 'the other side' ('the enemy', 'the apartheid state') which was almost as anonymous to me as I was to them?

And I tried to draw him out, to get him to explain his background. He said his parents were decent people who had brought him up with a strong sense of honour, especially his mother. He had been a good student at University and on graduating he had decided that the military was the career for him. He had advanced rapidly, he told me with pride, he had been an excellent soldier, and then he had been recruited for special operations.

I did not wish to pre-empt the interrogation of the Truth Commission—I just wanted him to say as much as he was willing to say. He would have seen the dossier on me. It would have shown that I had been in exile in Mozambique, neighbouring on South Africa, working on the reconstruction of the Mozambique legal system, that although I had been an active member of the African National Congress and especially of its Constitutional Committee, I was not involved in any underground activity or military or intelligence work. Yet they had chosen me—had tried to eliminate me. Why? Because I was an intellectual and challenged their claim that no political system could be found to enable black and white to live together as equals in South Africa? Every intellectual dreams of being taken seriously, but not that seriously...

We spoke for about two hours. He looked at me almost with a measure of jealousy. Here he was sitting in my chambers, beautiful pictures on the walls, I was a judge of the Constitutional Court, the highest court in the country, and he was now a demobilized soldier, with a torn past and a fragmented future. He had not even been given a golden handshake, but a brass one—a modest sum of money compared to what the retiring generals had received. Yet he had been willing to invest his energies, his intelligence, maybe even his life, for his country, for apartheid. And now he had been cast aside. He too had injuries—he told me he had been shot in the leg and walked with a slight limp. He seemed petulant: I was on the Court and he was unemployed. We could have gone on eyeing each other and talking forever.

I stood up and said: 'Henri...(a cheap emotion surged in me, I was tempted to say—I cannot shake your hand, you can see what happened to the hand I once upon a time used for greeting)...normally, if someone comes to my office, when I say goodbye I shake that person's hand, but I can't shake your hand. I can't now. Go to the Truth Commission, tell your story, help the country, do something for South Africa and then perhaps we can meet again.' When he walked back to the security door he was without the upright soldier's posture he had had before, and looked uncomfortable, uneasy, and sad. He went through the door, I said farewell and he disappeared.

The Truth and Reconciliation Commission

Something like thirty Truth Commissions have been created in various parts of the world, yet none have had the impact of the South African one—not for better, not for worse. None have been so profoundly influential in the countries where they functioned, none have attracted so much international attention. What was so special in South Africa?

The first point is that our Truth Commission was not the brainchild of a group of wise people sitting around a table deciding that in order to deal with the injustices of the past, the country should set up a Truth Commission. The pressure for the Commission in fact emerged from very intense and specific internal South African needs.

The story starts with a meeting of the National Executive Committee of the African National Congress in August 1993, about eight months before the first democratic elections were due to be held. It was a passionate meeting, sharp, uncomfortable. The issue was how to respond to a report of a commission of enquiry set up by the ANC to investigate violations of human rights committed by ANC cadres in Angolan camps during the liberation struggle. The report stated that ANC security had captured a number of persons suspected of having been sent by Pretoria to assassinate the leadership and generally create havoc. While interrogating them—this was in the early 1980s—the guards and security officials had frequently behaved in a barbaric way.

As I have said, the organization itself had investigated the matter, changed the whole security apparatus, and in 1985 created a code of conduct which was in effect a code of criminal law and procedure. It was probably the only liberation movement in the world that had ever produced a code of that kind, with tribunals, prosecution, defence counsel all being established, offences defined, charges put, evidence led and challenged, with a system of appeals. By and large, though not completely, the violations of human rights stopped. Now it was 1993, ten years later, and the armed struggle phase was over. Yet the violations had taken place. What did the ANC as a movement think about the unacceptable things that ANC members had done during the course of the struggle? The report was emphatic: certain people should be called to account. The eighty members of the National Executive Committee were now discussing what to do.

Some people said forcefully: we set up the Commission, it has reported, we have to follow through. And others responded with equal vehemence: how can we do that, we were fighting a freedom struggle in difficult conditions in the bush in Angola, the enemy was ruthless and would stop at nothing, we had young people quite untrained in interrogation techniques, they did their best, they protected the leadership, how can we punish them now?

The reply then came: we are a freedom movement, we were fighting for justice—if justice does not exist inside our own ranks, if we do not hold to these values, if we simply use the techniques of the enemy, we are like the enemy, we are no better than they are; the people have accepted great suffering because they believe in our cause—you cannot fight for life and be the enemy of life at the same time. Pallo Jordan, who is now a Minister in the government stood up, and in his well-elocuted, high-pitched voice said, 'Comrades, I've learnt something very interesting today. There is such a thing as regime torture, and there is ANC torture, and regime torture is bad and ANC torture is good; thank you for enlightening me!' And he sat down.

The house was divided on the issue. Profound moral issues were at stake, not the sort that could be decided by a show of hands. Eventually somebody stood up and asked the simple question: what would my mother say? The figure of 'my mother' represented an ordinary, decent, African working-class woman, not sophisticated but with a good heart and an honest understanding of people and the world—a person whose hard life experiences had promoted a natural sense of honour and integrity. He then answered himself: my mother would say there is something crazy about the ANC. Here we are examining our own weaknesses and faults and exposing our nakedness to the whole world, which maybe has to be done. But in the meantime all those villains on the other side, who have been doing these things and worse for decades and centuries, murdering, mutilating and torturing our people, are getting away scot-free. Nobody is examining what they did, and what some of them are still doing. Are we so perverse and introspective, are we so obsessed with our own moral health that we do not even think about the pain and the damage caused by the other side, by people who are now getting away completely without any kind of punishment, without taking responsibility for anything? What kind of freedom movement are we when we are so insensitive to the pain of millions of ordinary people? Where is the balance? Where is the justice?

It was at that moment that Professor Kader Asmal stood up and said: what we need in South Africa, the only answer, is a

Truth Commission. Only a Truth Commission can look at all the violations of human rights on all sides from whatever party. Human rights are human rights, they belong to human beings, whoever they might be. Any torture or other violation has to be investigated on an even-handed basis across the board, not just by one political movement looking at itself, but on a national level, with national resources and a national perspective.

He was clearly right. That was the moment when a political decision was taken that if an ANC government came to power after the elections, and it was assumed that it would, a Truth Commission would be set up that would examine all abuses of human rights—from whatever quarter—in the final years of apartheid.

A second crucial ingredient also emerged from the innards of South African experience. The negotiators had signed the draft text of a new, non-racial democratic Constitution. We thought it was all over. We had worked out a two-stage process of constitution-making, involving an elected Constitutional Assembly, modelled very much on the Indian experience, which would draft a final Constitution. We had agreed on thirty-four principles that would be binding on the Constitutional Assembly. We thought that all that remained was to hold the elections. I had in fact gone to London to report on the new constitutional arrangements to a Catholic civil society body that had given us much support over the years. As the negotiations had progressed our accommodation had improved, ending up in the airport Holiday Inn. But now I was back in grass-roots lodgings near Kings Cross, with little communication with the world. An embarrassed messenger from my host organization knocked on the door as I was about to sleep and handed me a telex he said was urgent. It was from ANC headquarters saying that there was a crisis requiring urgent attention. Apparently the security forces had said to the leadership that they had been promised an amnesty by President De Klerk, and that they had loyally protected the negotiations process, they were fully prepared to safeguard the elections against a bombing campaign intended to destroy the whole transition process, and they would defend the new Government and the new constitutional order. But not, they added, if afterwards they faced jail for their actions in support of the previous government—that was asking too much. They were not threatening a coup, but simply to resign *en masse* if no amnesty was granted.

This created a problem for the ANC leadership. The promise of amnesty had been given by President De Klerk, not by themselves. At the same time, they acknowledged that the security forces had loyally protected the negotiation process against many assaults from various right-wing sources. They were also aware that ANC security was not in a position itself to defend the election process, as they simply did not know who the bombers were. Generations of us had dreamed of elections on the basis of 'one person, one vote', of a new constitutional order where everyone would be equal, and where the crimes of the past could not be repeated. If the elections were severely disrupted, the dream would be destroyed and racial violence would continue. The security forces were not themselves aiming a gun at the transition process, but were simply saying that they should be given some recognition for enabling the democratic process to advance. At the same time, to grant them blanket amnesty because of their support for the constitutional process would have negated the principle of institutional and personal accountability. There was no spare paper in my bed-room so I wrote my response on the back of the telex. Why not, I proposed, link amnesty to a truth commission: there would be no blanket amnesty, but each individual who came forward and acknowledged what he or she had done, would receive indemnity to that extent.

This suggestion was followed, and in this way the Truth Commission and the amnesty process were linked on an individualized basis. That turned out to be the foundation of the South African Truth Commission and the basis for its unprecedented success. It meant that the perpetrators of violations of human rights, the torturers, the killers, had a motive to come forward and reveal what they had done. In exchange, the country would learn the truth. It was not through show-trials, bribery, or torture that they would confess; it was not through using the methods that the old regime had used—keeping people in solitary confinement, making them stand for days on end, electric shock torture, and thus forcing compliant, emotionally destroyed witnesses to testify. It was through voluntary confession, induced by the guarantee of amnesty.

Three elements turned out to be necessary for the process to work well. Firstly, it was important that the Truth and Reconciliation Commission (TRC) function within a sound legal framework in a clear constitutional setting. Thus, the Constitution itself provided for a right to amnesty for offences committed in the course of the political conflicts of the past, but stated that the right could only be enjoyed under terms and conditions to be established by the new parliament. The new parliament then went on to provide that a Truth Commission would be the mechanism for determining on a case-by-case basis how amnesty could be granted.

Secondly, although the drive for the TRC might have come primarily from the new Government, the details could not be unilaterally imposed. Some measure of consensus, however incomplete and reluctant, had to be achieved. A year was spent on the enabling legislation. It was a strenuous period of consultation and debate, of trying to bring in all the different interested parties and civil society with a view to securing the best mechanisms, balance and confidence in the process. The role of civil society organizations turned out to be particularly important. Like many human rights bodies throughout the world, they were unhappy that any amnesty at all should be granted for atrocious conduct (sometimes those who have not been through the fires themselves are more unrelenting than those who have suffered directly). If, however, the process was to go ahead, they insisted that it should be conducted in the open so that the public could know exactly what was happening. I had in fact recommended *in camera* hearings for those claiming amnesty, believing that only in this way would those responsible for the abusive conduct come forward. I was wrong. Fortunately the civil society insistence on open proceedings prevailed over my unduly cautious approach.

Thirdly, it was vital to staff the TRC with individuals of calibre, of standing, of manifest integrity, who had not themselves been directly involved in the conflicts of the past. This did not mean finding 'neutrals'. Anybody who claimed to have been neutral in the face of apartheid would not have been the right person to deal with allegations of torture. What was needed was not neutrality, but impartiality. This required participation of persons who were passionate about justice and human rights, but impartial in terms of evaluating the roles and functions that any particular persons, groups, parties, or formations had played in supporting or undermining respect for human dignity. This meant they would look at what had happened in the ANC camps with the same degree of objectivity and impartiality that they would use in examining the massive violations committed over long periods of time by the security forces. And in Archbishop Desmond Tutu, chairperson of the TRC, an outstanding individual with such qualities was found. After a complex screening process which covered individuals from a wide range of social, cultural and religious backgrounds, other personalities of manifest capacity and calibre were selected.

The Commission was divided into three sections, each functioning separately with different personnel. The first was the structure that heard the testimony of victims of gross violations of human rights. One must recall that the system of apartheid itself violated human rights and had been condemned as a crime against humanity. All the laws in terms of which people were identified by race, forced to carry passes, evicted from land, denied access to education, public facilities and the vote—all of these violated human rights. But they were not the subject of the TRC investigation. Nor were the harsh security laws under which people were detained in solitary confinement without trial. The TRC investigated acts which were crimes even under apartheid law.

These were violations of human rights that were so ugly and gross that they had been hidden and denied even by those who had openly supported race domination. The tortures, the assassinations, the people who had disappeared, the cross-border commando raids where people had been kidnapped or killed, had all been illegal in terms of South African law, even in terms of draconian apartheid security legislation. This was the focus of the TRC. The aim was not to investigate apartheid, which as a system had been condemned by humanity and totally repudiated by the new Constitution. Rather, the objective was to examine the crimes that had been committed and hidden during the apartheid period, mainly those committed in defence of apartheid, but also violations of human rights perpetrated in the struggle against apartheid.

Tutu called this section, over which he in fact presided, the one for the 'little people'. At last those in the townships, the communities, the rural areas, whose voices had never been heard, would be allowed to tell of their grief, their pain, and their loss. People like myself had appeared on television, written books about our experiences, travelled around the world, and spoken to many audiences about what had happened to us. But there were thousands and thousands of people who not only had suffered the immediate shock of violence to their bodies, or the pain of the loss of a son, daughter, mother, or father, but the lasting additional sorrow of having had to keep this hurt secret all this time. Something like ten thousand people testified in various parts of the country as to what had happened to them and their families, and another ten thousand sent in written testimonies.

Judges do not cry. Archbishop Tutu cried. It was not a court of law in the sense of an austere institution making highly formalized findings. It was an intensely human and personalized body, there to hear in an appropriately dignified setting what people had been through. There were comforters sitting next to the witnesses—in a court of law no one is there to help the witness, to pat the shoulder, or provide water or tissues when the person weeps. Frequently the sessions would start with a song in beautiful African harmony intended to give a sense of encouragement and support to everybody present. Or it could begin with prayers. And thereafter people spoke and spoke in all the regions and in all the languages of the country. The testimony was televised, and thus the nation became witness to what had happened and heard the stories directly from the mouths of the persons concerned. Those who spoke were not complainants in a court denouncing accused persons in the dock. Nor were they litigants demanding damages for themselves, so that the greater the loss, the greater the sum they would receive. Neither punishment nor compensation was at issue. They simply used the opportunity to speak the truth and have their pain acknowledged.

A five-volume report summarizing and analysing their testimony was published. It is a brilliant document, which even includes photographs and excerpts from some of the most poignant aspects of the testimony. It is not a dry governmental report, but a passionate memorial that resonates with the emotion of the hearings themselves. In addition, it contains serious reflection on how evil behaviour is condoned and spreads itself, and on what institutional mechanisms and what kind of culture are necessary to prevent its re-appearance. That was one of the greatest objectives of the Commission—not simply to allow the pain to come out, but to explain the conditions that permitted gross injustice to flourish so as to ensure that these things do not happen again.

And no one escaped the enquiry. Business, where were you? Business was making money, business was co-operating directly with the security forces, supplying explosives, trucks, and information. The press, where were you? There were some brave newspapers and wonderful journalists, but by and large the press was racist in its structure and fearful in its thinking, and went along with the stories about these terrorists, how dangerous they were, and how they had got what was coming to them. Thus, a business journal carried an editorial saying I had lived by the sword and no one could complain if I died by the sword. And the stories about people slipping on a piece of soap, falling out of the window, tripping down a flight of stairs, were carried by the press as if they might well be true, together with masses of disinformation which created a climate in which freedom fighters were demonized and could more easily be tortured or killed.

The legal profession, the judges, where were you? We judges, old and new, had hard debates in our own ranks. The strongest view was that the judiciary had contributed substantially to injustice by enforcing racist laws and showing an unacceptable lack of vigilance in the face of accusations of torture and abuse. When the executive took sweeping powers to lock up and detain people without trial, and brought to court witnesses who had endured months and years of solitary confinement, this was treated as normal procedure. There were some judges, again, who showed outstanding poise and courage, proving that even in the most constrained of circumstances, choices in favour of justice always exist. They used what little space was available to them to maintain the greatest traditions of the law, and I am proud to say that some of them became my colleagues on the Constitutional Court. But the great majority were compliant with the unjust laws enforced in an unjust manner. In the end, leaders of the judiciary sent a document to the TRC which acknowledged the failure of the judiciary as an institution to protect basic rights during the apartheid period.

The Reparations Committee was completely separate. It received reports from the first Commission, and ensured that each victim received monetary compensation on a lump-sum basis. The pain and suffering of a whole generation, not just those who testified, could not be measured. And funds could not be taken away from schooling, health, and land reform. But some kind of material compensation was given to all the victims who came forward. Yet there were understandable complaints about the amounts given and about the manner in which they were given. At the same time there was overwhelming support for the many dignified re-burials of people executed or tortured to death. In my view, however, not enough was done to create living memorials, scholarships for the children of those who died, streets renamed, gardens created, and monuments designed—not grandiose 'monumental' monuments, but ones as simple as the people themselves and as searing, sharp and evocative as the pain they had suffered.

The third section of the Commission, the one with the most difficult task, was the Amnesty Committee. It had two judges in each panel, and was the one that came closest to being like a court of law. Yet whereas a criminal court normally decides whether a person should go to jail, here it was deciding just the opposite, whether someone should be freed from prosecution. Because personal liberty was at stake, something like due process of law was applied, but without the strict rules of evidence and formal charges of a trial. A number of spectacular, terrible matters were dealt with.

Chris Hani, one of the first guerrillas who rose to be commander of Umkhonto we Sizwe, the military wing of the ANC, and then became general secretary of the Communist Party of

South Africa, was a popular hero. He went jogging during an Easter break in the period when we were still negotiating a new Constitution. As he returned home, somebody got out of a car, put a pistol to his head, and gunned him down. It turned out that his killer was an extreme right-winger from Poland who had been living for some years in South Africa, working with a far-right grouping in the country. A neighbour gave the identity of the motorcar, the police captured him, and, almost literally, a smoking gun was found. One of the ironies of our history is that it was the ANC's opposition to capital punishment that saved him and a co-conspirator from execution and enabled them subsequently to apply for amnesty. Should they be given amnesty or not? The Committee decided that the killers had withheld too much of the truth, and refused amnesty. They were prosecuted and given life sentences.

Then there was a group that was part of the Winnie Mandela football team. Winnie—brave, isolated, combative, passionate, warm, embracing and, some would say, capable of destroying anybody or anything in her way—gathered around herself a group of people who committed mayhem and created great conflict with the local ANC. This was in the late apartheid period when Nelson Mandela was still in jail. People died cruel deaths. It was not Winnie who applied for amnesty, but members of the football team, claiming that Mama Mandela had been the one who had ordered them to do these things. Should they receive amnesty? These were hard, searing, painful South African questions, requiring hard, searing, painful South African answers. Our Truth Commission was harsh, raw. It gave rise to much controversy and invited deep reflections. Thus, the killers of Steve Biko, a particularly brave and forthright leader, were refused amnesty because they had held back on the truth. Yet the persons who murdered Ruth First and Jenny Schoon with letter bombs were granted amnesty on the basis that however horrible the assassinations, the perpetrators had met the amnesty criteria.

Knowledge and Acknowledgement

I will share some of my personal reflections on the Truth Commission. The first deals with the difference between knowledge and acknowledgement, a concept passed on to me by Stan Cohen, who in turn had heard it explained to him by Thomas Nagel. Knowledge involves possessing information, being aware of facts. There was in reality an enormous amount of knowledge about repression in South Africa, but hardly any acknowledgement of what the cost was in human terms. Acknowledgement involves an acceptance not only of the existence of a phenomenon, but of its emotional and social significance. It presupposes a sense of responsibility for the occurrence, an understanding of the meaning that it has for the persons involved and for society as a whole.

One way of looking at the TRC process was to see it as a means of converting knowledge into acknowledgement. First came acknowledgement of the pain of the past. The fact that thousands of people had suffered was common knowledge—that the state had cracked down on them, that injuries had been sustained, that people had died in detention. Yet the human and personal dimension had been extruded, the pain shut out. That bare information became transformed when you saw individuals on the television, when you gave them a name and heard their stories at first hand. It was also specially meaningful for those who testified, who returned home and later saw themselves on television. As a result of the TRC, the private sorrow and grief of tens of thousands was publicly acknowledged in an embracing and personalized way. Another form of acknowledgement emerged from the perpetrators themselves. They had to come forward openly in front of the television cameras, owning up to their crimes. Finally, there was acknowledgement by the whole country that these things happened and can happen again— that we needed to fit all these facts together into some kind of significant pattern which would enable us to understand their genesis and do what we could to minimize any possibility of their recurrence.

The publicity that the civil society groups had demanded turned out to be the key to the enormous impact that the TRC had on national and international consciousness. The tears, the voices, the stiffness, the cries of sorrow, were all unmistakably recognizable. A vast and intense drama was enacted in front of the eyes of millions of viewers and readers. People asked themselves what they had done or not done, and what they should have done in the circumstances.

Four Categories of Truth

I was profoundly puzzled, as a lawyer and a judge, by many features of the TRC. They mainly concerned how we were to understand the concept of truth. The question asked in jest almost two thousand years ago still had to be answered: What is truth? I am not trained in the sciences of epistemology and ontology, and so I invented four rough categories of truth that I found helpful: observational truth, logical truth, experiential truth, and dialogic truth.

Observational truth, whether in natural or social science, involves narrowing the field to a particular frame and excluding all variables except those to be measured. In a court of law we pose and answer a particular question in a defined field such as whether a certain person is guilty of wrongfully and intentionally killing another at a particular time and in a particular manner. You identify, circumscribe and verify. That is observational truth—it is detailed, it is focused.

Logical truth is the generalized truth of propositions, the logic inherent in certain statements. It is arrived at by deductive and inferential processes, in the end, I suppose, drawing its strength from the capacity of language to encode abstract relationships between things in the world. Much of the law is concerned with finding the connections between observational truth and logical truth, that is, with setting observational truth in a logical framework.

Experiential truth is of a different order. It is the understanding gained from being inside and part of a phenomenon. It is the truth that we are all exposed to by living through a particular experience. I first came across the concept when reading MK Gandhi's *My Experiments with Truth*. I was puzzled by that title. These were not experiments as I understood the term; experiments were what we did at school when testing hypotheses with Bunsen burners and flasks of liquid in controlled conditions. Gandhi started without an hypothesis. He was testing himself, not an idea or the world out there. The process was to immerse himself thoughtfully and sensitively in certain experiences, and then draw conclusions from what he had lived through. An honest, objective interrogation is central to the process, together with a capacity to stand objectively outside yourself, and to look at your subjective experience in a truly unprejudiced way. Such experiential truth is deep and profound. Yet it embarrasses us in courts of law—we try to exclude it, we see it as subjective, irrelevant. We claim that all we want is the objective truth, what we call 'the facts'.

Finally, there is what I call dialogical truth. It is a truth based on interchange between people. We all have different experiences of reality, and diverse interests and backgrounds that influence the meaning of those experiences for ourselves. The debate between many contentions and points of view goes backwards and forwards, and a new synthesis emerges, holds sway for a while, is challenged, controverted, and a fresh debate ensues. The process is never-ending—there is no finalized truth.

Observational truth is definitive within its narrow frame; experiential truth is open-ended but it is personal to the individual concerned; logical truth is objective, generalized, impersonal and not dependent on external verification; and dialogical truth embodies elements of all of these, but assumes and thrives on the notion of a community of many voices and multiple perspectives. In the case of South Africa, there is no uniquely correct way of describing how the gross violations of human rights took place; there is no single narrator who can claim to have a definitive perspective that must be the right one.

Thus, the experience of the victims of violations of human rights was intense and real but was no more exclusively true than the experience of the perpetrators or the experience of the press or the experience of the judges. This is not to eliminate standards for evaluating conduct. The TRC notion presupposes measuring human conduct according to how it shows or denies respect for human dignity. It also assumes that people always have choices and must be held accountable for what they do. What dialogic truth implies is that the most pertinent description and the most meaningful evaluations of the phenomenon under question result from putting together all these layers of truth, different experiences and variety of voices. The Truth Commission itself was not one homogenous entity with twelve, fifteen or seventeen robotic heads, all thinking, seeing and experiencing things in the same way. The narration and evaluation in the report was itself the product of dialogue between different members of the commission. Tutu had his own particular confessional, personal, and experiential approach. His deputy had similar values but a different life experience. The other commissioners were from different backgrounds, reflecting diverse historical and cultural experiences. They composited rather than simply aggregated their different perspectives and evaluations. That is the way and the life of dialogic truth.

The strength of the TRC, and the reason why it resonated so powerfully, was that it was based essentially on dialogue—on hearing all the different viewpoints, on receiving inputs from all sides. It was not a case of people coming in as prosecutors and saying: We represent the state, we are going to examine and get the truth out of you. The state did not get the truth out of anybody. It did not work that way. An increasingly rich and true story emerged from a multiplicity of voices and perspectives. Then the TRC, itself a variegated body, had the function of trying to find the language, mode of presentation, and way of telling the story that would be as meaningful and convincing as possible.

The problem I had afterwards was: why does so little truth come out in a court of law, when so much emerged from the TRC? It poured out in huge streams, with overwhelming and convincing force. Many of the details and some of the assessments might have been challengeable, but the basic sweep was incontrovertible. One of its huge achievements was to eliminate denial. Not even the most ardent defenders of the old order could deny the evil that had been done in its name. Court records, on the other hand, are notoriously arid as sources of information. Outside the specific details under enquiry, you learn little. The social processes and cultural and institutional systems responsible for the violations remain uninvestigated.

The answer to this puzzle must lie in the differing objectives of the respective enquiries. Courts are concerned with accountability in a narrow individualized sense. They deal essentially with punishment and compensation. Due process of law relates not so much to truth, as to proof. Before you send someone to jail there has to be proof of responsibility for the wicked details charged. When the penalties and consequences are grave and personalized, you need this constrained mode of proceeding. The nation wishing to understand and deal with its past, however, is asking much larger questions: How could it happen, what was it like for all concerned, how can you spot the warning signs, and how can it be prevented from occurring again? If you are dealing with large episodes, the main concern is not punishment or compensation after due process of law, but to achieve an understanding and acknowledgement by society of what happened so that the healing process can really start. Dialogue is the foundation of repair. The dignity that goes with dialogue is the basis for achieving common citizenship. It is the equality of voice that marks a decisive start, the beginning of a sense of shared morality and responsibility.

Ultimately we can only have full reconciliation when conditions have been created where the full dignity of all South Africans is respected and everyone has equal life chances. But repair of inter-personal relations has in the meanwhile been vastly facilitated by the TRC. I think that was a great lesson for our country, and possibly for the world. We did need an International Criminal Court functioning according to due process of law, where virtue sought unequivocally to trounce evil. But we also required a wide and flexible range of programmes which allowed for other means of coming to terms with trauma and violence, where the format was not that of inquisitor and accused, but that of interlocutors trying to find common ground. All had an equal chance to speak. Some achieved relief through being heard, others accepted shame when acknowledging cruel conduct; but they were speaking to each other, not trying to kill one another. Indeed, what both the Constitution-making process and the TRC had in common was recognition of the need for fierce antagonists to look into the eyes of former enemies and discover elements of a common humanity there. If the Constitution itself was the product of achieving dignity and security through dialogue, it followed that it should be interpreted in a way that fostered resolving disputes through dialogue. And the impact of the TRC went beyond helping us deal with the rest. The principle of getting people to look each other in the eye, and not shrink from dealing with the most grievous problems, became further entrenched in our culture.

Furthermore, as will be seen from the *AZAPO* case and the *Dikoko* case (at p 95 and p 99), the themes of apology and mediation seeped deeply into my consciousness, and influenced the way I felt the judiciary should function.

Truth and Reconciliation

In an immediate sense, there has been little direct reconciliation. Few of the torturers were forgiven directly by their victims—very few. People felt raw, angry, upset, the more so because not many of the perpetrators had been able to show much spontaneous human emotion. Yet there were exceptions. There was a man from the white community blinded by an ANC bomb in Pretoria. Abubaker Ismail, the person who was responsible for the bomb, applied for amnesty, explaining that as part of the freedom struggle, his unit had put the bomb near a military target. He said he regretted very much that he had been compelled to fight with these methods, and felt especially sorry about the injuries caused to the victim. And the blind person put out his hand, shook the hand of Ismail and said: I understand why you did it, you were fighting for freedom, that was your motivation, we must move forward now.

We had other cases in South Africa just like that. It was not unique, but it was unusual. For the most part, the hurt is still there. Instead of coming forward and speaking from the heart and crying and being open, most of the perpetrators came in neatly pressed suits, expressing tight body language, with their lawyers next to them, and read prepared statements as though they were in a court of law. Their admissions were important but tended to be limited to a factual acknowledgement of unlawful conduct coupled with a rehearsed apology, rather than encompassing an emotional and convincing acknowledgement of wrongdoing. There is a huge generosity, particularly amongst African people, waiting to come out, but it can only express itself if there is a counterpart of openness and honesty of feeling on the part of the perpetrators. Just as even in this highly marketized world we still have a right to altruism—so even in a legal and moral universe based on accountability, there is a right to forgive. The problem is that the right to forgive can only be enjoyed if the perpetrators acknowledge their wrongfulness.

Yet even allowing for all these serious limitations in the reconciliation process, I believe that the basic objective of laying the foundations of national reconciliation was largely achieved. On an individual basis and between all communities we have a long way to go, but at the national level we now, for the first time, have a single narrative, a common history of the most painful moments of the recent past. You cannot have a country with different memories and expect a sense of common citizenship to grow. You cannot have a white history and a black history that have nothing to do with each other, except that they overlap in time and place. You have to have a single, broad, commonly accepted narrative of the country's history. In that sense, although we are still living in an unfair land, where facilities and life opportunities are not the same for black and white, we inhabit a much less divided country than the one we occupied before. As Americans put it—we are coming all to be on the same map, or at least beginning to assemble there. That has been a huge gain.

It should be remembered, too, that accountability can take many forms. Even punishment should not be seen simply as sending people to jail. The persons who appear on television and say 'We cut up the body and threw the pieces to the crocodiles afterwards', do not get off scot-free. They are punished by exposure, punished by shame. They see the families of the victims in a setting where they no longer exercise total power over them. They look into their eyes as equals. Afterwards, they go home, and have to look into the eyes of their neighbours, their children, their families. Once upon a time they received handshakes and promotions, now they are abandoned and repudiated. Many received treatment for post traumatic stress disorder. Their bleak faces served as warnings to all in future: nothing remains secret, the truth will out.

Many bodies of disappeared persons were recovered. We received the truth for the first time of how Steve Biko was killed, how the community leaders known as the Cradock Four were murdered—years of inquest and inquiry had produced nothing. So we gained an enormous amount both of knowledge and of acknowledgement. The price was to offer indemnity to those who came forward with the truth. Yet prosecution without evidence would have been difficult and we would not have known whom to prosecute for what. I think the country grew stronger for the process.

How could we prevent these things from recurring in future? Part of the answer was to convince the security forces that they could not expect secrecy and cover-up in the future. Security forces must never feel that they can rely on being protected by the state, come what may. The TRC achieved this, at least for our generation. Another part of the answer was to develop a new culture in the country at large. The TRC process sank profoundly into the consciousness of the nation. Hopefully the report will one day be integrated into school curricula and its conclusions will irradiate

South African thinking generally. Evil and cruelty must be seen for what they are; protecting the state against some imagined terrible evil from outside cannot justify it violating moral norms and committing great evils. A further safeguard comes from having strong institutions in place dedicated to defending fundamental human rights. Our Constitution gives great significance to such institutions. One of them is the Constitutional Court, of which I have the honour to be a member.

The Constitutional Court

We have built a new Constitutional Court right in the heart of what had been Johannesburg's most notorious prison. In a highly visible way it symbolizes the 'never again' principle coupled with the redemptive possibilities of national life. It happens to have a strong connection with India, and not simply because Gandhi had been imprisoned there. We had an international competition for a new court building: 600 people bought the competition brochure and 180 entries were received, 40 from outside South Africa. The chairperson of the jury was Charles Correa, the Mumbai and MIT architect. He was chosen because we felt he had the right philosophy for the kind of building we wanted—not a copy of a North American building transplanted to South Africa, but an edifice that came out of our culture, located itself in our history, and responded to our light, physical texture, topography, and needs.

Geoffrey Bawa, a distinguished architect from Sri Lanka, was another member of the jury. Monika Correa, who accompanied her husband Charles, presented us with a luminous tapestry she had made showing a banyan tree firmly rooted in the ground, yet floating in space. The symbol of the Constitutional Court is a large tree under which the people shelter—they protect the tree, and the tree protects the people. Her tapestry has a prominent place in our court, and represents a direct Indian presence there. But the connection with India is not simply a physical one. The site that we chose for the court building is the Old Fort prison. We say, with mixed feelings of satisfaction and shame, that South Africa possesses the only prison in the world where both Gandhi and Mandela were locked up. And those who are familiar with the story of Gandhi in South Africa will know that many of his most intense experiments with truth took place precisely in that prison. His decision not to take salt when he saw that the Indian prisoners received salt with their food while African prisoners did not, was made there, and generated the idea of voluntarily giving up physical pleasures so as to understand the experience of living like those treated as the humblest in society. Sadly, it was South Africa that provided him with that rich experience. When Indian prisoners were ordered to wear the prison caps that African prisoners were obliged to wear, he did not object, but said he would wear the cap with a sense of pride. And when in 1914 he returned to India, he took the cap with him, and it became the symbol of the Indian freedom struggle. Our Court now stands on the site of the prison from which the Gandhi cap emanated.

We needed a new building for our new Court and our new democracy, but kept the old prison structures. The prisons are there, surrounding the Court, with one prison staircase incorporated into the building itself and the prison bricks cladding the Court chamber. The Court represents not only the important 'never-again' principle of constitutional democracy, but also the theme of survival, of hope, of the triumph of courage and humanity over despair and cruelty. The terrible negative energy of the past was converted into positivity for the future. We wanted the new building to be a simple edifice, where justice would be accessible, friendly and warm. If I walk into a magistrate's court in South Africa today, I feel guilty, and I am a judge in the highest court in the land! There is something about standard court architecture that proclaims authority, that says 'Beware, the state is on top of you'. Yet our court does not express power, it restrains power. Our job is to defend the new Constitution. It is to ensure that all public power is exercised in terms of the processes laid down by our Constitution and in keeping with the precepts and values enshrined in it.

It is in relation to values that so much of Gandhi comes through to us. The underlying values of our new democracy are spelt out in our Bill of Rights and in the very concept of equal citizenship, which presupposes not only negative protections against abuse by public power, but also affirmative claims to a decent and dignified life for all. The Court is expressly required to promote the values of an open and democratic society. Such a society acknowledges the equal worth and dignity of each of its members, the most exalted and the humblest, and respects the fact that people are different, sometimes superficially, sometimes deeply. These are Gandhian ideals.

Yet it is not only the spirit of Gandhi that can be found in our Constitution, but the philosophy of Nehru. It is no accident that the title of Mandela's autobiography 'Long Walk to Freedom' was taken from a phrase by Nehru—there is no easy walk to freedom. The experiences of the Indian freedom struggle and the processes used to accommodate diversity in a democratic national framework, had a profound influence on Mandela's generation and are reflected in our new constitutional dispensation. So we get themes about the institutionalization of democracy from one great Indian personality, and the spirit of compassion and self-denial from another. These were two enormous inputs, communicated across the Indian Ocean not just by writings but through the experiences of struggle and imprisonment of scores of South Africans who worked directly with the two great Indian leaders.

Other influences came from other continents, from the rest of Africa, from Europe, from North and South America. Universalism and globalization are diametrically opposed concepts. The universalism of human rights comes not from the globalized imposition of one set of values on all humanity. Human rights are not exported from one centre to the rest of the world. Rather they are the product of the unabating struggle and shared idealism throughout the world. The international principles emerge as the distillation of a universal quest for human dignity. In this way, the aspirations of generations of freedom fighters in our country and abroad, over the ages, have come to be embodied in the terms of the Constitution that I as a judge on the Constitutional Court have sworn to defend.

Afterword

I was at a party in Johannesburg, feeling quite light-headed after a heavy year's work in court. The party was at the home of a friend whose father had been one of the first to be assassinated by apartheid hit-squads; as a child she had cradled her dad as he lay dying. To this day she does not know who actually killed him, but she has got on with her life and has now become a film-maker of repute. It was an end-of-year party for the actors and crew of a gritty and intelligent soap opera of which she was one of the directors.

In the midst of the music and hilarity I heard a voice calling out, 'Hello, Albie!' I turned around and saw a familiar face smiling at me, looking very happy. The person spoke again, 'Hello, I am Henri, do you remember me?' At first, the name did not register. The speaker went on, 'Remember, I came to...'. And I remembered, 'You came to my office; you were going to the TRC...'.

The music was throbbing, the people were dancing around. We moved to a corner so that we could hear each other better. He was beaming. I asked him what had happened. He told me he had written to the TRC, giving them all the information he could, and had applied for amnesty in relation to six different matters. And afterwards, he said, he had spent hours with Sue and Bobby and Farook, all of whom had been in Mozambique in those hard years, answering their questions on behalf of the TRC. He was speaking on first-name terms about persons I knew well, all freedom fighters who had been in Mozambique, and he used their names with great affection and enthusiasm.

Then he stopped talking, looked at me and said, 'You told me that afterwards...maybe...?' And I responded, 'Yes, Henri, I said to you that afterwards if you co-operated with the Truth Commission, if you did something for South Africa, maybe we could meet again...I've only got your word for it, but I can see from your face you are telling the truth.'

And I put out my hand and I shook his hand.

He went away elated. I moved away and almost fainted into the arms of a friend of mine. I heard later from the puzzled organizers of the party that he had left suddenly and gone home and cried for two weeks.

The *Azapo* Case

*The genesis of the Truth and Reconciliation Act is eloquently expressed in
further excerpts from Ismail Mahomed's judgment in the AZAPO case.*

MAHOMED DP:

[T]hose who controlled the levers of state power began to
negotiate a different future with those who had been imprisoned, silenced, or driven into exile in consequence of their
resistance to that control and its consequences. Those negotiations resulted in an interim Constitution committed to a
transition towards a more just, defensible and democratic
political order based on the protection of fundamental
human rights. It was wisely appreciated by those involved
in the preceding negotiations that the task of building such
a new democratic order was a very difficult task because of
the previous history and the deep emotions and indefens-
ible inequities it had generated; and that this could not be
achieved without a firm and generous commitment to reconciliation and national unity.

This fundamental philosophy is eloquently expressed in the
epilogue to the Constitution which reads as follows:

National Unity and Reconciliation

This Constitution provides a historic bridge between the past of
a deeply divided society characterised by strife, conflict, untold
suffering and injustice, and a future founded on the recognition
of human rights, democracy and peaceful co-existence and development opportunities for all South Africans, irrespective of
colour, race, class, belief or sex.

The pursuit of national unity, the well-being of all South African citizens and peace require reconciliation between the people of South Africa and the reconstruction of society.

The adoption of this Constitution lays the secure foundation for the people of South Africa to transcend the divisions and strife of the past, which generated gross violations of human rights, the transgression of humanitarian principles in violent conflicts and a legacy of hatred, fear, guilt and revenge.

These can now be addressed on the basis that there is a need for understanding but not for vengeance, a need for reparation but not for retaliation, a need for ubuntu but not for victimisation.

In order to advance such reconciliation and reconstruction, amnesty shall be granted in respect of acts, omissions and offences associated with political objectives and committed in the course of the conflicts of the past. To this end, Parliament under this Constitution shall adopt a law determining a firm cut-off date, which shall be a date after 8 October 1990 and before 6 December 1993, and providing for the mechanisms, criteria and procedures, including tribunals, if any, through which such amnesty shall be dealt with at any time after the law has been passed.

With this Constitution and these commitments we, the people of South Africa, open a new chapter in the history of our country.

Pursuant to the provisions of the epilogue, Parliament enacted what is colloquially referred to as the Truth and Reconciliation Act.

For a successfully negotiated transition, the terms of the transition required not only the agreement of those victimized by abuse but also those threatened by the transition to a 'democratic society based on freedom and equality'. If the Constitution kept alive the prospect of continuous retaliation and revenge, the agreement of those threatened by its implementation might never have been forthcoming, and if it had, the bridge itself would have remained wobbly and insecure, threatened by fear from some and anger from others. It was for this reason that those who negotiated the Constitution made a deliberate choice, preferring understanding over vengeance, reparation over retaliation, ubuntu over victimisation.

The result, at all levels, is a difficult, sensitive, perhaps even agonising, balancing act between the need for justice to victims of past abuse and the need for reconciliation and rapid transition to a new future; between encouragement to wrongdoers to help in the discovery of the truth and the need for reparations for the victims of that truth; between a correction in the old and the creation of the new. It is an exercise of immense difficulty interacting in a vast network of political, emotional, ethical and logistical considerations. It is an act calling for a judgment falling substantially within the domain of those entrusted with lawmaking in the era preceding and during the transition period. The results may well often be imperfect and the pursuit of the act might inherently support the message of Kant that 'out of the crooked timber of humanity no straight thing was ever made'. There can be legitimate debate about the methods and the mechanisms chosen by the lawmaker to give effect to the difficult duty entrusted upon it in terms of the epilogue. We are not concerned with that debate or the wisdom of its choice of mechanisms but only with its constitutionality.

The erstwhile adversaries of such a conflict inhabit the same sovereign territory. They have to live with each other and work with each other and the state concerned is best equipped to determine what measures may be most conducive for the facilitation of such reconciliation and reconstruction. That is a difficult exercise which the nation within such a state has to perform by having regard to its own peculiar history, its complexities, even its contradictions and its emotional and institutional traditions. What role punishment should play in respect of erstwhile acts of criminality in such a situation is part of the complexity.

The *Dikoko* Case

A judicial plea by myself in a minority judgment for the remedy in defamation (libel) cases to move away from focusing on money awards towards encouraging apology.

SACHS J:

Damages awards in defamation cases...measure something so intrinsic to human dignity as a person's reputation and honour as if these were marketplace commodities. Unlike businesses, honour is not quoted on the Stock Exchange. The true and lasting solace for the person wrongly injured is the vindication by the Court of his or her reputation in the community. The greatest prize is to walk away with head high, knowing that even the traducer has acknowledged the injustice of the slur...

There is something conceptually incongruous in attempting to establish a proportionate relationship between vindication of a reputation, on the one hand, and determining a sum of money as compensation, on the other. The damaged reputation is either restored to what it was, or it is not. It cannot be more restored by a higher award, and less restored by a lower one. It is the judicial finding in favour of the integrity of the complainant that vindicates his or her reputation, not the amount of money he or she ends up being able to deposit in the bank...

The notion that the value of a person's reputation has to be expressed in rands in fact carries the risk of undermining the very thing the law is seeking to vindicate, namely, the intangible, socially constructed and intensely meaningful good name of the injured person. The specific nature of the injury at issue requires a sensitive judicial response that goes beyond the ordinary alertness that courts should be expected to display to encourage settlement between litigants. As the law is currently applied, defamation proceedings tend to unfold in a way that exacerbates the ruptured relationship between the parties, driving them further apart rather than bringing them closer together. For the one to win, the other must lose, the score-card being measured in a surplus of rands for the victor...

What is called for is greater scope and encouragement for enabling the reparative value of retraction and apology to be introduced into the proceedings. In jurisprudential terms, this would necessitate reconceiving the available remedies so as to focus more on the human and less on the patrimonial dimensions of the problem. The principal goal should be repair rather than punishment. To achieve this objective requires making greater allowance in defamation proceedings for acknowledging the constitutional values of *ubuntu-botho*...

Ubuntu-botho is more than a phrase to be invoked from time to time to add a gracious and affirmative gloss to a legal finding already arrived at. It is intrinsic to and constitutive of our constitutional culture. Historically it was foundational to the spirit of reconciliation and bridge-building that enabled our deeply traumatized society to overcome and transcend the divisions of the past. In present-day terms it has an enduring and creative character, representing the element of human solidarity that binds together liberty and equality to create an affirmative and mutually supportive triad of central constitutional values. It feeds pervasively into and enriches the fundamental rights enshrined in the Constitution...

Ubuntu-botho is highly consonant with rapidly evolving international notion of restorative justice. Deeply rooted in our society, it links up with worldwide striving to develop restorative systems of justice based on reparative rather than purely punitive principles. The key elements of restorative justice have been identified as encounter, reparation, reintegration and participation. Encounter (dialogue) enables the victims and offenders to talk about the hurt caused and how the parties are to get on in future. Reparation focuses on repairing the harm that has been done rather than on doling out punishment. Reintegration into the community depends upon the achievement of mutual respect for and mutual commitment to one another. And participation presupposes a less formal encounter between the parties that allows other people close to them to participate. These concepts harmonise well with processes well known to traditional forms of dispute resolution in our country, processes that have long been, and continue to be, underpinned by the philosophy of *ubuntu-botho*...

Like the principles of restorative justice, the philosophy of *ubuntu-botho* has usually been invoked in relation to criminal law, and especially with reference to child justice. Yet there is no reason why it should be restricted to those areas. It has already influenced our jurisprudence in respect of such widely divergent issues as capital punishment and the manner in which the courts should deal with persons threatened with eviction from rudimentary shelters on land unlawfully occupied. Recently it was applied in creative fashion in the High Court to combine a suspended custodial sentence in a homicide case with an apology from a senior representative of the family of the accused, as requested and acknowledged by the mother of the deceased...

I can think of few processes that would be more amenable in appropriate cases to the influence of the affirming values of *ubuntu-botho* than those concerned with seeking simultaneously to restore a person's public honour while assuaging interpersonal trauma and healing social wounds. In this connection attention should be paid to the traditional Roman-Dutch law concept of the *amende honorable* . . .

Although *unbuntu-botho* and the *amende honorable* are expressed in different languages intrinsic to separate legal cultures, they share the same underlying philosophy and goal. Both are directed towards promoting face-to-face encounter between the parties, so as to facilitate resolution in public of their differences and the restoration of harmony in the community. In both legal cultures the centrepiece of the process is to create conditions to facilitate the achievement, if at all possible, of an apology honestly offered, and generously accepted . . .

The whole forensic mindset, as well as the way evidence is led and arguments are presented, is functionally and exclusively geared towards enlarging or restricting the amount of damages to be awarded, rather than towards securing an apology. In my view, this fixed concentration on *quantum* requires amendment. Greater scope has to be given for reparatory remedies . . .

It is noteworthy that in the context of hate speech the Legislature has indicated its support for the new remedy of apology. Thus the Equality Court is empowered to order that an apology be made in addition to or in lieu of other remedies. I believe that the values embodied in our Constitution encourage something similar being developed in relation to defamation proceedings. In the light of the core constitutional values of *ubuntu-botho*, trial courts should feel encouraged proactively to explore mechanisms for shifting the emphasis from near-exclusive attention to *quantum*, towards searching for processes which enhance the possibilities of resolving the dispute between the parties, and achieving a measure of dignified reconciliation. The problem is that, if the vision of the law remains as tunneled as it is today, parties will be discouraged from seeking to repair their relationship through direct and honourable engagement with each other. Apology will continue to be seen primarily as a tactical means of reducing damages rather than as a principled modality for clearing the air and restoring a measure of mutual respect...

Giving special emphasis to restoring the relationship between the parties does not, of course, imply that awards of damages should completely fall out of the picture. In our society money, like cattle, can have significant symbolic value. The threat of damages will continue to be needed as a deterrent as long as the world we live in remains as money oriented as it is. Many miscreants would be quite happy to make the most abject apology (whether sincere or not) on the basis that doing so costs them nothing—'it is just words'. Moreover, it is well established that damage to one's reputation may not be fully cured by counter-publication or apology; the harmful statement often lingers on in people's minds. So even if damages do not cure the defamation, they may deter promiscuous slander, and constitute a real solace for irreparable harm done to one's reputation...

What is needed, then, is more flexibility and innovation concerning the relation between apology and money awards. A good beginning for achieving greater remedial suppleness might well be to seek out the points of overlap between *ubuntu-botho* and the *amende honorable*, the first providing a new spirit, the second a time-honoured legal format. Whatever renovatory modalities are employed, and however significant to the outcome the facts will have to be in each particular case, the fuller the range of remedial options available the more likely will justice be done between the parties. And the greater the prospect of realising the more humane society envisaged by the Constitution...

The *Port Elizabeth Municipality* Case

*Extracts from my judgment in the Port Elizabeth Municipality case, where
the Court held that it would not be just and equitable to evict extremely
poor black families from shacks erected on white-owned land if mediation
had not first been tried.*

SACHS J:

It is not only the dignity of the poor that is assailed when homeless people are driven from pillar to post in a desperate quest for
a place where they and their families can rest their heads. Our
society as a whole is demeaned when state action intensifies
rather than mitigates their marginalization. Thus, the integrity
of the rights-based vision of the Constitution is punctured when
government action augments rather than reduces denial of the
claims of the desperately poor to the basic elements of a decent
existence. Hence the need for special judicial control of a process that is both socially stressful and potentially conflictual.

The phrase 'just' and equitable [used in the Prevention of
Illegal Eviction and Unlawful Occupation Act, known as PIE]
makes it plain that the criteria to be applied are not purely of the
technical kind that flows ordinarily from the provisions of land
law. The emphasis on justice and equity underlines the central
philosophical and strategic objective of PIE. Rather than envisage
the foundational values of the rule of law and the achievement of
equality as being distinct from and in tension with each other, PIE
treats these values as interactive, complementary and mutually
reinforcing. The necessary reconciliation can only be attempted

by a close analysis of the actual specifics of each case. The court is thus called upon to go beyond its normal functions, and to engage in active judicial management according to equitable principles of an ongoing, stressful and law-governed social process. This has major implications for the manner in which it must deal with the issues before it, how it should approach questions of evidence, the procedures it may adopt, the way in which it exercises its powers and the orders it might make...

The Constitution and PIE require that in addition to considering the lawfulness of the occupation the court must have regard to the interests and circumstances of the occupier and pay due regard to broader considerations of fairness and other constitutional values, so as to produce a just and equitable result. Thus PIE expressly requires the court to infuse elements of grace and compassion into the formal structures of the law. It is called upon to balance competing interests in a principled way and promote the constitutional vision of a caring society based on good neighbourliness and shared concern. The Constitution and PIE confirm that we are not islands unto ourselves. The spirit of *ubuntu*, part of the deep cultural heritage of the majority of the population, suffuses the whole constitutional order. It combines individual rights with a communication philosophy unifying motif of the Bill of Rights which is nothing if not a structured, institutionalized and operational declaration in our evolving new society of the need for human interdependence, respect and concern... *

---

* Justice Yvonne Mokgoro explained the meaning of ubuntu in a case where the Court declared capital punishment to be in conflict with the Bill of Rights, in the following manner:

   Generally ubuntu translates as 'humaneness'. In its most fundamental sense it translates as personhood and 'morality'. Metaphorically, it expresses itself in

The inherited injustices at the macro level will inevitably make it difficult for the courts to ensure immediate present-day equity at the micro level. The judiciary cannot itself correct all the systemic unfairness to be found in our society. Yet it can at least soften and minimize the degree of injustice and inequity which eviction of the weaker parties in conditions of inequity of necessity entails. As the authors of the minority judgment in the second abortion case in the German Federal Constitutional Court pointed out, there are some problems based on contradictory values that are so intrinsic to the way our society functions that neither legislation nor the courts can 'solve' them with 'correct' answers...

When dealing with the dilemmas posed by PIE, the courts must accordingly do as well as they can with the evidential and procedural resources at their disposal...

In seeking to resolve the above contradictions, the procedural and substantive aspects of justice and equity cannot always be separated. The managerial role of the courts may need to find expression in innovative ways. Thus one potentially dignified and effective mode of achieving sustainable reconciliation of the different interests involved is to encourage and require the parties to engage with each other in a proactive and honest

umuntu ngumunt ngabantu, describing the significance of group solidarity on survival issues so central to the survival of communities. While it envelopes the key values of group solidarity, compassion, respect, human dignity, conformity to basic norms and collective unity, in its fundamental sense it denotes humanity and morality. Its spirit emphasizes a respect for human dignity, marking a shift from confrontation to conciliation. In South Africa ubuntu has become a notion with particular resonance in the building of a democracy. It is part of our rainbow heritage, though it might have operated and still operates differently in diverse community settings. In the Western cultural heritage, respect and the value for life manifested in the all-embracing concepts of 'humanity' and 'menswaardigheid', are also highly priced. It is values like these that [the Constitution] requires to be promoted. They give meaning and texture to the principles of a society based on freedom and equality.

endeavour to find mutually acceptable solutions. Wherever possible, respectful face-to-face engagement or mediation through a third party should replace arms-length combat by intransigent opponents...

Compulsory mediation is an increasingly common feature of modern systems. It should be noted, however, that the compulsion lies in participating in the process, not in reaching a settlement. In South Africa, mediation or conciliation are compulsory in many cases before labour disputes are brought before a court. Mediation in family matters, too, though not compulsory, is increasingly common in many jurisdictions...

Thus, those seeking eviction should be encouraged not to rely on concepts of faceless and anonymous squatters automatically to be expelled as obnoxious social nuisances. Such a stereotypical approach has no place in the society envisaged by the Constitution; justice and equity require that everyone is to be treated as an individual bearer of rights entitled to respect for his or her dignity. At the same time those who find themselves compelled by poverty and homelessness to live in shacks on the land of others, should be discouraged from regarding themselves as helpless victims, lacking the possibilities of personal moral agency. The tenacity and ingenuity they show in making homes out of discarded material, in finding work and sending their children to school, are a tribute to their capacity for survival and adaptation. Justice and equity oblige them to rely on this same resourcefulness in seeking a solution to their plight and to explore all reasonable possibilities of securing suitable alternative accommodation or land...

Not only can mediation reduce the expenses of litigation, it can help avoid the exacerbation of tensions that forensic combat produces. By bringing the parties together, narrowing the areas of dispute between them and facilitating mutual give-and-take, mediators can find ways round sticking-points in a manner that the adversarial judicial process might not be able to do. Money that otherwise might be spent on unpleasant and polarising litigation can better be used to facilitate an outcome that ends a stand-off, promotes respect for human dignity and underlines the fact that we all live in a shared society...

In South African conditions, where communities have long been divided and placed in hostile camps, mediation has a particularly significant role to play. The process enables parties to relate to each other in pragmatic and sensible ways, building up prospects of respectful good neighbourliness for the future. Nowhere is this more required than in relation to the intensely emotional and historically charged problems with which PIE deals. Given the special nature of the competing interests involved in eviction proceedings launched under section 6 of PIE, absent special circumstances it would not ordinarily be just and equitable to order eviction if proper discussions, and where appropriate, mediation, have not been attempted.

S v M

The principles of restorative, rather than punitive justice have been developed most strongly in the area of juvenile justice. In a case that came to our Court, however, the rights of children had to be considered when it was not them, but their mother, who faced imprisonment. Found guilty of repeated credit card fraud while out on bail, the mother asked to be placed under corrective supervision outside of prison. In a judgment that was supported by the majority of my colleagues, I emphasized that in cases like this courts were constitutionally obliged to give special attention to the impact on children of the imprisonment of their primary care-giver. Paying attention to the combined effect of upholding the rights of her children and pursuing the objectives of restorative justice, the judgment opted for keeping the mother out of prison. Three of the ten judges disagreed on the facts, and would have sent her to prison with an opportunity for fairly early release for correctional supervision.

SACHS J:

Every child has his or her own dignity. If a child is to be constitutionally imagined as an individual with a distinctive personality, and not merely as a miniature adult waiting to reach full size, he or she cannot be treated as a mere extension of his or her parents, umbilically destined to sink or swim with them. The unusually comprehensive and emancipatory character of s 28 [in the Bill of Rights, dealing with the rights of children] presupposes that in our new dispensation the sins and traumas of fathers and mothers should not be visited on their children.

Individually and collectively all children have the right to express themselves as independent social beings, to have their own laughter as well as sorrow, to play, imagine and explore in their own way, to themselves get to understand their bodies, minds and emotions, and above all to learn as they grow how they should conduct themselves and make choices in the wide social and moral world of adulthood. And foundational to the enjoyment of the right to childhood is the promotion of the right as far as possible to live in a secure and nurturing environment free from violence, fear, want and avoidable trauma...

[An] advantage of correctional supervision [for a mother facing imprisonment] is that it keeps open the option of restorative justice in a way that imprisonment cannot do. Central to the notion of restorative justice is the recognition of the community rather than the criminal-justice agencies as the prime site of crime control. Thus, our courts have observed that one of its strengths is that it rehabilitates the offender within the community, without the negative impact of prison and destruction of the family. It is geared to punish and rehabilitate the offender within the community leaving his or her work and domestic routines intact, and without the negative influences of prison.

[It] is necessary to place in the balance the following facts. M has shown a meritorious aptitude to organise her life productively and pursue successful entrepreneurial activities during the past seven years. There is no suggestion on the papers that she has behaved dishonestly during this period. She has a fixed address and has been stated to be a suitable candidate for correctional supervision. It is in the public interest to reduce the prison population wherever possible. To compel her to undergo further imprisonment would be to indicate that community resources are incapable of dealing with her moral failures. I do not believe that they necessarily are. Nor do I believe that the community should be seen simply as a vengeful mass uninterested in the moral and social recuperation of one of its members. M has manifested a will to conduct herself correctly. As the courts have pointed out, persons should not be excluded from correctional supervision simply because they are repeat offenders.

None of the above should be seen as diminishing the seriousness of the offences for which she was properly convicted. Nor should it be construed as disregarding the hurt and prejudice to the victims of her fraud. Nevertheless, I conclude that in the light of all the circumstances of this case M, her children, the community and the victims who will be repaid from her earnings, stand to benefit more from her being placed under correctional supervision than from her being sent back to prison.

4

Reason and Passion

Although the voice of my judgments was my own, the intellectual well from which my thoughts were drawn was the same as that used by all my colleagues, namely, the Constitution. In one way or another all my colleagues on the Court had confronted and challenged the deep indignities and injustices that flowed from apartheid. The Constitution was anti-racist to its core. Our generation were in fact the originators of its text. The Constitution itself presupposed the existence of an activist Constitutional Court engaged with finding principled and implementable responses to the deep problems of racism, sexism and inequality in our country. Its express language also invited us to locate ourselves within the mainstream of forward-looking international legal thought.

Yet however much we drew from the same source, and however convivial my colleagues were, there is something inherently lonely in being a judge. My sense of isolation was intensified by the knowledge that my judgments almost always came out in a manner and style rather different from that used by my colleagues. Fortunately, solace was to come to me from two unexpected sources. The first was the discovery that another judge, and a most distinguished one at that, working in a completely different social and historical context, had been driven by exactly the same intellectual compulsions as those that seemed to impel me along. He was Justice William Brennan of the United States Supreme Court.

When lecturing in the USA I would ask my audience to guess the names of the two United States Supreme Court Justices whom I tended to quote most often in my judgments? The answer was Robert Jackson, for the incomparably telling way he communicated deeply thoughtful reasoning, and William Brennan, for the measured manner in which his cadences conveyed his progressive judicial vision. A listener told me he had written a biography of Brennan and presented me with a copy. In it, I came across a lecture which Brennan had given in honour of Justice Benjamin Cardozo, which eloquently set out what could have been my philosophy. He started by pointing out that Cardozo had awakened America to the human reality of the judicial process by showing that judging could not properly be characterized as simply the application of pure reason to legal problems nor, at the other extreme, as the application of the personal will or passion of the judge. Rather there was a complex interplay of forces—rational and emotional, conscious and unconscious—by which no judge could remain unaffected. It was Brennan's thesis that this interplay of forces, this internal dialogue of reason and passion, did not taint the judicial process, but was in fact central to its vitality, and particularly true in constitutional interpretation. With this I wholeheartedly agree.

Brennan pointed out that at the beginning of the twentieth century the focus on reason had become so tight that all else had been excluded from view, and the legal community had become convinced that a broader focus would gravely threaten the legitimacy and authority of the judicial branch. In his view, however, a greater threat lay in the legal community's failure to recognize the important role that qualities other than reason had to play in the judicial process. In ignoring these qualities, the judiciary had deprived itself of the nourishment essential to a healthy and vital rationality. Brennan referred to these qualities under the rubric of 'passion', a word he chose deliberately because it was general and conveyed much of what seemed at first blush to be the very enemy of reason. By 'passion' he meant the range of emotional and intuitive responses to a given set of facts or arguments, responses which often sped into our consciousness far ahead of the lumbering syllogisms of reason. After quoting from Cardozo that law had its piercing intuitions, its tense apocalyptic moments, he observed that the well-springs of imagination lay less in logic than in the realm of human experience—the realm in which law ultimately operated and had meaning. Sensitivity to one's intuitive and passionate responses, and awareness of the range of human experience, was therefore not only an inevitable but a desirable part of the judicial process, an aspect more to be nurtured than feared.

Brennan concluded by saying that the open-ended nature of a written constitution, and the different ways of reconciling competing principles and passions, placed an enormous responsibility on the judge. The task of constitutional interpretation, particularly from the perspective of the Supreme Court, was daunting. No matter now much one had studied or thought about the Constitution, the weight of responsibility that came with the job of Supreme Court Justice could not be fully anticipated. The struggle for certainty, for confidence in one's interpretative efforts, was real and persistent. Although judges might never achieve certainty, they had to continue in the struggle, for it was only as each generation brought to bear its experience and understanding, its passion and reason, that there was hope for progress in the law. Once more I must express my agreement.

My second source of solace arrived in a totally surprising way. When I had the novel and delightful experience of seeing people in other jurisdictions quoting from my judgments, I noticed that the passages they chose were precisely those that had emanated from the most subliminal regions of my consciousness in the least judicial of circumstances. I will give some examples, and explain these circumstances.

It started with a statement in a judgment of mine on capital punishment. It was to the effect that if the killer is executed, he or she achieves a perverse moral victory because by killing the killer, the state reduces public abhorrence at the idea of the deliberate taking of human life. In a preface to a book on capital punishment written for a British and international audience, Professor Andrew Rutherford quoted that statement. And I remembered how I had come to write it. Our very first case had dealt with the constitutionality of capital punishment. The issues had raised powerful thoughts and haunting emotions on all sides. With a view to allowing my thoughts and emotions to settle, I would give myself the occasional treat of immersion in a long warm bath. And it was during one such somnolent soak that the formulation eventually quoted by Professor Rutherford had surfaced, unbidden and complete, into my mind. It had been the least rationally-induced, the least deliberately thought-through phrase in the whole of my judgment, and yet it had travelled the best.

Then, a little while later Lord Steyn of the British House of Lords Judicial Committee sent me an extract from a judgment he had just given dealing with the technical issue of how the reverse onus (burden of proof) in a statute impacts on the presumption of innocence. The reverse onus requires that once certain facts are proved, the accused person must demonstrate that other facts exist to excuse him or her from liability. Did this violate the presumption of innocence? The quotation he used was to the effect that there is a paradox that lies at the heart of the presumption of innocence in a criminal trial: the more harmful the crime and the greater the public need to secure a conviction, the more important it is to uphold the presumption of innocence for the individual accused. (The full quotation appears in *The Paradox at the Heart of Criminal Procedure*, see p 120.) Now this too was one of those thoughts, initially startling but ultimately obvious, that had come to me while lying inert and only half-awake in the bath.

I suspect that if diligent researchers one day went through the scraps of paper on which I have jotted down occasional ideas, they would find many of them with the ink smudged by water-drops. And what astonished me was that it was precisely these unforced, undirected, jotted-down thoughts that had travelled the best. Of course, they had not in fact generated themselves. The groundwork had been laid by hard, rational investigation for weeks and months, by reading hundreds of pages of law reports, textbooks, and journal articles, by debates with my colleagues so that my head overflowed with a jumble of unsorted ideas and formulations. Yet only when I had been close to being in what my Buddhist friends would call a transcendental meditational state, would these formulations emerge, as if from nowhere. It was as if the discovery, justification, persuasion, and preening had all coalesced in one spontaneous moment of creation.

The same thing happened in a case dealing with the right of prisoners to vote. At the time I had wondered why it was that I had felt particularly strongly about the subject, and it was when my mind was apparently switched off that sudden enlighten-ment had come. It was not simply that voting was a democratic right that every citizen had—I wrote, after leaping out of the bath—but that the hard-won right to vote touched deeply on the dignity of all human beings; voting united the highest and the humblest in a single polity, and declared quite literally that every person counted. (The full quotation appears in *The Meaning of the Vote*, see p 122.) This underlying rationale had appeared fully formed in my head, making sense out of the jumble of compet-ing notions that until then had lodged there unreconciled. And the conceptual discovery had been inseparable from the rhet-orical language in which it had been expressed. Later, this was the one passage of my judgment that came to be referred to in a majority judgment of the Canadian Supreme Court in a similar case. No Cartesian reasoning had been involved in its creation. And yet it had travelled across the ocean to a court that I hap-pened to admire very much.

I must stress that other judges on the Constitutional Court have been quoted by courts abroad, and I have never discussed with them the circumstances in which new ideas have come to them. I suspect, however, that if pushed, each one would have recalled off-guard moments when fresh concepts had suddenly presented themselves: while gardening, or running, or doing the laundry, or walking on the mountain, or even when at the wheel of a car on a monotonous journey. And on reflection, I do remember a colleague mentioning that a clinching argument in his judgment had come to him while he had been in the shower that morning.

Archimedes is said to have had his 'eureka' moment in his bath, but I doubt that there is anything special about immersing oneself in hot water to promote creativity. Indeed, I have now become more of a shower person, and would not like to think that the jurisprudence of my Court has suffered unduly as a result. But it so happened that the first three times I was cited in foreign jurisdictions, the formulations had all come to me at moments when my brain had been least engaged in hard legal reasoning.

I draw two conclusions from this. The one is obvious, namely, that passionate life experiences will inevitably insinuate themselves to grapple profoundly with dispassionate reasoning when legal pronouncements are being prepared. The other is less obvious. It is that the effect of life experience on the judicial mind will not be linear and predictable. Thus, growing up in an actively anti-religious home could have made me innately disdainful of claims made for protection of religious conscience in the public sphere. Yet if anything, the actual experience of being a non-believing child in a religious school environment seems to have predisposed me strongly towards supporting rights of conscience. I think this tendency is exemplified by another bath-induced judgment of mine which travelled to the House of Lords in London. (See *Religious Exemption from General Law*, at p 123.) It emphasized the duty on the state to accommodate, where reasonably possible, exemptions for religious believers from general law.

The Paradox at the Heart
of Criminal Procedure

*Speech by Lord Steyn in the case of R v Lambert [2001] UKHL 37, Judicial
Committee of the House of Lords.*

LORD STEYN:

In H M Advocate v McIntosh, P.C. (5/2/2001) Lord Bingham of
Cornhill recently referred to the judgment of Sachs J of the
South African Constitutional Court in *State v Coetzee* [1997] 2
LRC 593. It is worth setting out the eloquent explanation by
Sachs J of the significance of the presumption of innocence in
full [para 220 at 677]:

> There is a paradox at the heart of all criminal procedure in that
> the more serious the crime and the greater the public interest in
> securing convictions of the guilty, the more important do consti-
> tutional protections of the accused become. The starting point of
> any balancing enquiry where constitutional rights are concerned
> must be that the public interest in ensuring that innocent people
> are not convicted and subjected to ignominy and heavy sentences
> massively out-weighs the public interest in ensuring that a par-
> ticular criminal is brought to book... Hence the presumption of
> innocence, which serves not only to protect a particular individual
> on trial, but to maintain public confidence in the enduring integ-
> rity and security of the legal system. Reference to the prevalence
> and severity of a certain crime therefore does not add anything
> new or special to the balancing exercise. The perniciousness of
> the offence is one of the givens, against which the presumption
> of innocence is pitted from the beginning, not a new element to
> be put into the scales as part of a justificatory balancing exer-
> cise. If this were not so, the ubiquity and ugliness argument could

be used in relation to murder, rape, car-jacking, housebreaking, drug-smuggling, corruption...the list is unfortunately almost endless, and nothing would be left of the presumption of innocence, save, perhaps, for its relic status as a doughty defender of rights in the most trivial of cases.

The Meaning of the Vote

How should one approach a claim by prisoners that they be allowed to vote in General Elections: are they authors of their own misfortune, or are they being denied a fundamental right? This is an extract from a judgment that I wrote for the Court which decided that prisoners could not be deprived of the right to vote through an administrative decision, but only through an Act of Parliament compatible with the Constitution. See August v Electoral Commission and Others (1999).

SACHS J:

Universal adult suffrage on a common voters' roll is one of the foundational values of our entire constitutional order. The achievement of the franchise has historically been important both for the acquisition of the rights of full and effective citizenship by all South Africans regardless of race, and for the accomplishment of an all-embracing nationhood. The universality of the franchise is important not only for nationhood and democracy. The vote of each and every citizen is a badge of dignity and personhood. Quite literally, it says that everybody counts. In a country of great disparities of wealth and power it declares that whoever we are, whether rich or poor, exalted or disgraced, we all belong to the same democratic South African nation; that our destinies are intertwined in a single interactive polity. Rights may not be limited without justification and legislation dealing with the franchise must be interpreted in favour of enfranchisement rather than disenfranchisement.

Religious Exemption from
General Law

How far must democracy go in allowing members of religious communities to be exempted from general law? Speech by Lord Walker in the Judicial Committee of the House of Lords in the case of R v Secretary of State for Education and Employment and others ex parte Williamson and others [2005] UKHL 15.

LORD WALKER:

Your Lordships were referred to a recent case before the Constitutional Court of South Africa, *Christian Education South Africa v Minister of Education* (2000) 9 BHRC 53, which raised essentially the same issue as is now before the House, but in a rather different context. The context was different because of the different terms of the South African Constitution and the different historical and social background, to which the Constitutional Court attached particular importance. Nevertheless, I have found the judgment of the Court, delivered by Sachs J, very helpful, especially the general discussion at pp 68–70, paras 33–35. Sachs J said at para 35:

> The underlying problem in any open and democratic society based on human dignity, equality and freedom in which conscientious and religious freedom has to be regarded with appropriate seriousness, is how far such democracy can and must go in allowing members of religious communities to define for themselves which laws they will obey and which not. Such a society can cohere only if all its participants accept that certain basic norms and standards are binding. Accordingly, believers cannot

claim an automatic right to be exempted by their beliefs from the laws of the land. At the same time, the state should, wherever reasonably possible, seek to avoid putting believers to extremely painful and intensely burdensome choices of either being true to their faith or else respectful of the law.

5

Laughing Matters

All is very still and calm and without movement or voices or muscular activity. I am wrapped in complete darkness and tranquillity. If I am dead I am not aware of it, if I am alive I am not aware of it, I have no awareness at all, not of myself, or of my surroundings, not of anyone or of anything.

'Albie...' through the darkness a voice, speaking not about me but to me, and using my name and without that terrible urgency of all those other voices '...Albie, this is Ivo Garrido speaking to you...' the voice is sympathetic and affectionate, I know Ivo, he is an outstanding young surgeon and a friend '...you are in the Maputo Central Hospital...your arm is in a lamentable condition ...' he uses a delicate Portuguese word to describe my arm, how tactful the Mozambican culture is compared to the English one, I must ask him later what that word is '...we are going to operate and you must face the future with courage.'

A glow of joy of complete satisfaction and peace envelops me, I am in the hands of Frelimo, of the Mozambique Government, I am safe.

'What happened?' I am asking the question into the darkness, my will has been activated in response to hearing Ivo's voice, I have a social existence once more, I am an alive part of humanity.

A voice answers, close to my ears, I think it is a woman's '...a car bomb...' and I drift back, smiling inside, into nothingness.

I am elsewhere and other. There is a cool crisp sheet on me, I am lying on a couch, aware that I have a body and that I can feel and think and even laugh to myself, and everything seems light and clean and I have a great sense of happiness and curiosity. This is the time to explore and rediscover myself. What has happened to me, what is left of me, what is the damage? I am feeling wonderful and thinking easily in word thoughts and not just sensations, but maybe there is internal destruction...

Let me see...A joke comes back to me, a Jewish joke from the days when we Jews still told jokes to ward off the pains of oppression and humiliation, from when I was still a young student and my mountain-climbing friend had a new joke for me each week, and I smile to myself as I tell myself the joke, and feel happy and alive because I am telling myself a joke the one about Himie Cohen falling off a bus, and as he get up he makes what appears to be a large sign of the cross over his body.

A friend is watching in astonishment. 'Himie,' he says 'I didn't know you were a Catholic.' 'What do you mean, Catholic?' Himie answers. 'Spectacles...testicles...wallet and watch.' My arm is free and mobile and ready to respond to my will. It is on the left side and I decide to alter the order a little, I am sure Himie would not mind in the circumstances. Testicles...My hand goes down. I am wearing nothing under the sheet, it is easy to feel my body. My penis is all there, my good old cock (I'm alone with myself and can say the word) that has involved me in so much happiness and so much despair and will no doubt lead me up hill and down dale in the future as well, and my balls, one, two, both in place, perhaps I should call them testes since I am in hospital. I bend my elbow, how lovely it is to be able to want again, and then be able to do what I want; I move my hand up my chest, what delicious self-determination, what a noble work of art is man...Wallet...My heart is there, the ribs over it seem intact, the blood will pump, the centre of my physical being, the part you take for granted is okay, I am fine, I will live and live robustly. Spectacles...I range my fingers over my forehead, and cannot feel any craters or jagged pieces, and I know I am thinking clearly, the darkness is now feather-light and clean, unlike the heavy, opaque blackness of before. Watch...my hand creeps over my shoulder and slides down my upper arm, and suddenly there is nothing there...so I have lost an arm, Ivo did not say which one, or even that they were going to cut it off, though I suppose it was implicit in his words and it's the right one, since it is my left arm that is doing all the feeling...So I have lost an arm, that's all, I've lost an arm, that's all. They tried to kill me, to extinguish me completely, but I have only lost an arm. Spectacles, testicles, wallet and watch. I joke, therefore I am.

This is a time for laughter, the listener participating in the story by means of almost continuous and celebratory laughter. I will enjoy doing the narration and [Jacob Zuma who has been sent by the ANC leadership to greet me after my discharge from hospital] will get the pleasure from egging me on to even richer and more comic correctness, counterpointing my reportage with a melodic accompaniment of rising and falling laughter.

Slowly I take Zuma through the hospital portion of the story, of hearing Ivo Garrido's voice and his exquisitely polite word for the state of my arm (huge laughter) and then his statement about operating and my having to face the future with courage (quieter laughter this time), and my comment at the relief I felt at being in the hands of Frelimo (appreciative laughter, high marks for being a good comrade at all times and for telling the story in a gracious and non-boastful way).

I launch into the final portion '…what do you mean, Catholic? … spectacles, testicles, wallet and watch.' Zuma doubles up and yells with laughter, his mouth wide open, his head rolling back and then coming down again, his eyes full of sympathetic mirth. I feel moved by the situation, by the intense interaction between us. This is what the ANC is, we do not wipe out our personalities and cultures when we become members, rather we bring in and share what we have, Zuma's African-ness, his Zulu appreciation of conversation and humour is mingling with my Jewish joke, enriching it, prolonging and intensifying the pleasure. [W]e are close, yet we do not have to become like each other, erase our personal tastes and ways of seeing and doing things, but rather contribute our different cultural inputs so as to give more texture to the whole. This is how one day we will rebuild South Africa, not by pushing a steamroller over the national cultures, but by bringing them together, seeing them as the many roots of a single tree, some more substantial than others, but all contributing to the tree's strength and beauty.

Laughter in Court

Laughter in Court is one thing. Laughter in the thought of the Court is another. Sometimes the feeblest joke from the bench is met with roars of dutiful laughter from counsel and spectators. I suspect that it is not just obsequiousness that is involved, but rather the anxiety that Freud wrote about in his examination of wit and the unconscious. Archbishop Tutu always gets responsive gurgles when he tells an audience that God has a sense of humour. Once more it is the release of anxiety that provokes the mirth. But, if the Lord has a sense of humour, does the Law? Are there anxieties in the law and public life that are best released by laughter? This is a question I dealt with in the *Laugh It Off* case (see p 130).

The *Laugh It Off* Case

In this matter the Court held that the parodied use of a trademark on a T-shirt should not be interdicted, because the detriment to the owner's property rights was small and far outweighed by free speech rights. In a separate concurring judgment I dealt specifically with the role of laughter in a democratic society. Excerpts follow.

SACHS J:

Does the law have a sense of humour? This question is raised whenever the irresistible force of free expression, in the form of parody, meets the immovable object of property rights, in the form of trade mark protection. And if international experience is anything to go by, it would seem that far from providing clear guidance, court decisions on the topic have been as variable as judicial humour itself.

In the present matter a graduate of a course in journalism decided to do battle with a number of corporate giants, calling his enterprise Laugh it Off and arming himself with T-shirts bearing parodied images and words brazenly pilfered from his opponents. One of his victims, South African Breweries [SAB], saw one of its well-known trademarks reproduced on T-shirts for public sale. The words 'Black Label' and 'Carling Beer' which accompanied the logo were transformed into 'Black Labour' and 'White Guilt'. In smaller lettering the slogans, 'America's Lusty Lively Beer' and 'Brewed in South Africa' were converted into 'Africa's Lusty Lively Exploitation Since 1652, No Regard Given Worldwide'. SAB did not laugh. Instead it went to the Cape High Court and sought, and obtained, an interdict restraining distribution of the T-shirts.

On appeal, the Supreme Court of Appeal [SCA] was equally unamused, holding that it was unfairly detrimental to SAB to link its protected imagery with imputation of racial exploitation, particularly if the objective was to sell T-shirts. Accordingly, the future sale of the T-shirts was, and remains, interdicted. The result of this double forensic defeat was paradoxically that while the trade name Laugh it Off achieved national and international fame, Laugh it Off itself faced looming insolvency. The joke now being on it, it appeals to this Court.

At the heart of this matter lies the legal dilemma posed by the fact that Laugh it Off utilised the SAB brand, not adventitiously, but deliberately and precisely in order to challenge SAB's use of branding. It went further. It employed the enemy's brand to denounce the power of branding in general, and to confront the employment of trademark law, in our country as elsewhere, to suppress free speech. It was a calculatedly risky activity, with the sense of irreverence and provocation being intrinsic to the enterprise. If parody does not prickle it does not work. The issue before us, however, is not whether it rubs us up the wrong way or whether Laugh it Off's provocations were brave or foolhardy, funny or silly. The question we have to consider is whether they were legally and constitutionally permissible. I believe they were eminently so, and give my reasons.

Parody is inherently paradoxical. Good parody is both original and parasitic, simultaneously creative and derivative. The relationship between the trademark and the parody is that if the parody does not take enough from the original trade mark, the audience will not be able to recognise the trade mark and therefore not be able to understand the humour. Conversely, if the parody takes too much it could be considered infringing, based upon the fact that there is too much theft and too little originality, regardless of how funny the parody is.

Parody is appropriation and imitation, but of a kind involving a deliberate dislocation. Above all, parody presumes the authority and currency of the object work or form. It keeps the image of the original in the eye of the beholder and relies on the ability of the audience to recognise, with whatever degree of precision, the parodied work or text, and to interpret or 'decode' the allusion; in this sense the audience shares in a variety of ways the creation of the parody with the parodist. Unlike the plagiarist whose intention is to deceive, the parodist relies on the audience's awareness of the target work or genre; in turn, the complicity of the audience is a sine qua non of its enjoyment.

In a society driven by consumerism and material symbols, trade marks have become important marketing and commercial tools that occupy a prominent place in the public mind. Consequently, companies and producers of consumer goods invest substantial sums of money to develop, publicise and protect the distinctive nature of their trademarks; in the process, well-known trademarks become targets for parody. Parodists may then have varying motivations for their artistic work; some hope to entertain, while others engage in social commentary, and finally others may have duplicitous commercial aspirations. Rutz states that:

> Often laughter is provoked not at the expense of the original work and its author, but at the dislocation itself. The public may find pleasure in recognising the parody's object; on the other hand,

reactions may be anger or shock, depending on the context in which the parody is set....

The question to be asked is whether, looking at the facts as a whole, and analysing them in their specific context, an independent observer who is sensitive to both the free speech values of the Constitution and the property protection object-ives of trademark law, would say that the harm done by the parody to the property interests of the trademark owner out-weighs the free speech interests involved. The balancing of interests must be based on the evidence on record, supple-mented by such knowledge of how the world works as every judge may be presumed to have. Furthermore, although the parody will be evaluated in the austere atmosphere of the court, the text concerned [whether visual or verbal or both] should be analysed in terms of its significance and the impact it had [or was likely to have], in the actual setting in which it was communicated...

The sole member of Laugh it Off, Justin Nurse, states that Laugh it Off is and continues to be a very small concern oper-ating on a shoestring budget. The way it has operated thus far has been to prepare limited runs of T-shirts, to set up a web-site, and from time to time to hold comedy events where these T-shirts are promoted.

Laugh it Off explains the logic behinds its use of T-shirt lam-poons as follows. Brands are omnipresent, and invade every aspect of our private and public space. They entrench them-selves in modern cultural consciousness by their self-made associations with certain lifestyles, ambitions, appeal to emo-tion, etc. Branding often has very little to do with the product itself. Thus Black Label beer tastes completely different all over the world, but has a similar brand. In South Africa the branding has nothing to do with actual taste and quality of the beer. It links the consumption of beer and particularly Black Label to manliness, sporting prowess and even sexual prowess:

- Carling Black Label is projected as something that is enjoyed by 'men' around the world. This clearly intends to convey that masculinity can be confirmed by drinking Black Label;
- Carling Black Label is a 'lusty, lively beer';
- Carling Black Label drinkers have or will acquire, one assumes, 'a big one';
- Carling Black Label drinkers get more at the end of the day.

Laugh it Off avers that the Black Label man is clearly intended to be a particular type, and if you want to be such a man, you should use your hard earned money to buy and drink Black Label beer. The love affair with America, and all things American (for example, township youth are attracted to the hip-hop culture prevalent in American inner cities), is also relied upon—almost as a fallacious 'appeal to authority'. The affidavit made in its support claims that:

> We live in a society where business and culture occupy the same space. It is here that the debate starts to arise, as the corporates try to make their brands South African culture icons—and yet, when they achieve this and their icon is commented on, they hide behind a set of rules (trade mark and copyright laws) that were surely not intended for the purpose of stifling cultural expression. It is fair to say that brands largely affect the way we act, and the decisions that we make…They are powerful, pervasive and persuasive. It is the nature of the brand's unquestionability that cannot stand…

Thus, when resistance to the self-ordained sanctity of the brand comes in the form of satirical T-shirts, corporate reaction is as if a crucifix had been smashed in a monastery in the 14th century. And indeed, Laugh it Off argues, the parallels between the church as an institution that defied any challenge or criticism for centuries, and big business's banner concept, the brand, defying challenge nowadays, could easily be drawn.

Laugh it Off sums up its position by claiming that it uses the vocabulary of our media-rich environment in a statement directed at a media-literate audience. This statement is made the more powerful because the vocabulary of our environment is the brand; in a media-saturated environment, the most evocative and powerful public discussion will use the vocabulary of that environment...

The evidence [in this case] indicates that everybody concerned with the T-shirts, whether as producer or consumer, knew that they were intended to poke fun at the dominance exercised by brand names in our social and cultural life. What united seller and buyer had nothing to do with beer, but was all about irreverence. The use of the trade mark was central to the project. This was not an example of a weapon parody being used exploitatively to 'get attention or to avoid the drudgery in working up something fresh'.

The balancing exercise in the present matter is therefore easily done. On the detriment side there is virtually no harm, if any at all, to the marketability of Carling Black Label beer. This is a case where the communication was far more significant than the trade. The trade was incidental to the communication. The objective of the enterprise, as clearly understood by all those involved, was to get a message across. The sale of the

T-shirts was necessary for sustainability. This was not a commercial activity masquerading as a free speech one. To say that the message could have been conveyed by means other than the use of the trade mark is to miss the point of the parody. The message lies precisely in the dislocated use of the trade mark. The challenge is to the power of branding in general, as exemplified by the particular trade mark. It is not to the particular beer as such. It should be stressed that the question is not whether the parody succeeds in hitting the mark. What matters is that it was part of a genuine attempt to critique the status quo in our society. The scales come down unequivocally on the side of Laugh it Off. In the felicitous phrase of an American judge, the evidence shows that in the present matter the parody was a take-off, not a rip-off, and the interdict should accordingly not have been granted.

I would like to add two considerations of special constitutional significance which I believe reinforce the conclusion to which I have come.

The first relates to the chilling effect that overzealously applied trade mark law could have on the free circulation of ideas. In this respect one must recognise that litigation could be a risky enterprise for a meritorious trade mark owner as well as the prankster. Applicants seeking to interdict the abusive use of their trade marks stand to be involved in lengthy litigation in which every manner of accusation could be made against them by persons from whom no costs could ultimately be recovered. Furthermore, any businesses seen as trying to block free speech could hardly be surprised if the media tended to champion their opponent's cause. Indeed, the very act of invoking the heavy machinery of the law might be regarded as being in conflict with the image of freedom, liveliness and good cheer associated with their product brand. Thus, in the present matter simply bringing the proceedings against Laugh it Off risked being more tarnishing of Carling Black Label's association with bonhomie and cheerfulness than the sale of 200 T-shirts could ever have done. The principle of litigator beware, however, faces any person contemplating legal action.

Of more significance from a constitutional point of view is the manner in which even the threat of litigation can stifle legitimate debate. Large businesses have special access to wealth, the media and government. Like politicians and public figures, their trade marks represent highly visible and immediately recognisable symbols of societal norms and values. The companies that own famous trade marks exert substantial influence over public and political issues, making them and their marks ripe and appropriate targets for parody and criticism.

Yet when applied against non-competitor parody artists, the tarnishment theory of trade mark dilution may, in protecting the reputation of a mark's owner, effectively act as a defamation statute. As such it could serve as an over-deterrent. It could chill public discourse because trade mark law could be used to encourage prospective speakers to engage in undue self-censorship to avoid the negative consequence of speaking— namely, being involved in a ruinous lawsuit.

This brings me to the second consideration of special constitutional import. The Constitution cannot oblige the dour to laugh. It can, however, prevent the cheerless from snuffing out the laughter of the blithe spirits among us. Indeed, if our society became completely solemn because of the exercise of state power at the behest of the worthy, not only would all irrelevant laughter be suppressed, but temperance considerations could end up placing beer-drinking itself in jeopardy. And I can see no reason in principle why a joke against the government can be tolerated, but one at the expense of what used to be called Big Business, cannot.

Laughter too has its context. It can be derisory and punitive, imposing indignity on the weak at the hands of the powerful. On the other hand, it can be consolatory, even subversive in the service of the marginalised social critics. What has been relevant in the present matter is that the context was one of laughter being used as a means of challenging economic power, resisting ideological hegemony and advancing human dignity. We are not called upon to be arbiters of the taste displayed or judges of the humour offered. Nor are we required to say how successful Laugh it Off has been in hitting its parodic mark. Whatever our individual sensibilities or personal opinions about the T-shirts might be, we are obliged to interpret the law in a manner which protects the right of bodies such as Laugh it Off to advance subversive humour. The protection must be there whether the humour is expressed by mimicry in drag, or cartooning in the press, or the production of lampoons on T-shirts. The fact that the comedian is paid and the newspaper and T-shirts are sold, does not in itself convert the expression involved into a mere commodity. Nor does the fact that parodists could have voiced their discontent by phoning into a talk show rather than employ the trade mark remove their protection. They chose parody as a means, and invited young acolytes to join their gadfly laughter.

A society that takes itself too seriously risks bottling up its tensions and treating every example of irreverence as a threat to its existence. Humour is one of the great solvents of democracy. It permits the ambiguities and contradictions of public life to be articulated in non-violent forms. It promotes diversity. It enables a multitude of discontents to be expressed in a myriad of spontaneous ways. It is an elixir of constitutional health.

6

Reason and Judgment

When I had been in solitary confinement I had wondered why it had been so difficult to be brave. Now as a judge I found myself puzzled by how difficult it was to be logical. Surely, I had thought, judgments wrote themselves: connect the principles with the facts, and the solution will flow like water from a rock struck by Moses. Yet in reality I laboured mightily, changed my arguments frequently, felt I was always on the verge of wrapping it all up and yet never quite able to achieve the certainty I craved. Neither life experiences nor application of dogmatic rules provided obvious answers. My secretary once informed me that her computer showed that I was proposing corrections to the twenty-sixth version of a draft, and that she and my law clerks sometimes conspired to hide my judgments in case I felt the urge to make yet one more change.

Yet if all that had been involved had been the application of simple logic to a defined situation, I should have got it in one. Is floundering, I wondered, a necessary part of the judicial function? Part of the answer to this question came during another dining-out seminar with professors from the University of Toronto. Jennifer Nedelsky had been a student of Hannah Arendt, who in turn had attempted to update to the twentieth century the writings of Immanuel Kant. The topic we discussed was the difference between reason and judgment. My recall of Jennifer's summary of Hannah Arendt's interpretation of Immanuel Kant's writing goes as follows: Reason was compelling, while judgment involved evaluation. Pure reason said that if A is bigger than B, and B is bigger than C, then A is bigger than C. Judgment, however, depended on weighing. To illustrate what judgment meant she gave the example of the difference between saying 'I like that picture', which does not involve judgment but is a purely subjective and incontrovertible statement of fact, and declaring 'That is a beautiful picture', which would be expressing a judgment that could be measured against agreed criteria as to what constituted beautiful art. The salient point was that by saying a picture was beautiful, the declarant presupposed that there were certain standards for evaluating beauty which were shared by members of the arts community within which the question of beauty was being discussed.

Something similar applies to a legal judgment. If I say a certain outcome is just or unjust, I am affirming that according to the principles, rules and standards that have come to be accepted in the legal community, the outcome is just or unjust. It is not enough that I believe passionately in my heart of hearts that the outcome is just or unjust. Delivering a judgment is a public act with public consequences. It is not dependent on personal taste, as a book review may and should be. Nor is it the product a purely logical exercise, like the solution to a mathematical problem. It is the outcome of an evaluation, of a weighing up of determinate factors in the light of agreed criteria. As a judge I must seek to convince readers of a judgment I write that the outcome is just. This requires me to refer to principles, rules and standards, to methods of reasoning and analysis, that are accepted by the community to whom my judgment is addressed.

Each member of that community might have his or her own subjective preferences and make his or her particular subjective evaluations. But the discourse between us must take on an objective character. It must relate to what constitutes a common understanding between us as to the rules and values governing the process.

Pure reasoning will always be one element of this legal discourse. But it will be only one of many. If justice could be dispensed in an automatic way as though by a legal vending machine, all we would have to do would be to feed in certain data, establish a hierarchy of legal rules, and the logic impressed into the mechanism of the machine would do the rest. Money would be saved, certainty would be achieved, equality of outcomes would be guaranteed, there would be no room for appeals and I would be out of a job.

Yet the very notion of judgment presupposes that there is no inevitable outcome. Judgment involves the conjugation of different elements which are weighed and evaluated according to certain agreed criteria to produce a decisive determination. In Jennifer's recall of Hannah Arendt's appreciation of Immanuel Kant's writings, a judgment does not purport to compel acceptance by the reader through a process of pure reasoning. Instead, it seeks to woo the consent of the reader by the persuasiveness of its argument. And part of what in turn defines the legal community whose acceptance is sought, is the very fact of its joint participation in the processes of understanding and applying the law. The legal community's identity and sense of self is thus predicated on its engaging with the principles, processes and values of the law. If Jennifer is correct, and I believe she is, then persuasion is not a gratuitous add-on to a closely-reasoned judgment. It is part of what justifies calling the ultimate judicial product something more than a 'decision', and referring to it as a 'judgment'.

Judging accordingly involves more than classifying and sorting. By its nature it presupposes an element of evaluation, whether at a flower show, a boxing match or a skating competition or in a court of law. Although the elements to be put into the scales are objectively defined, the weight given to each individually, and the overall balance to be achieved when all are put together, could vary from arbiter to arbiter. This makes it necessary to build in controls against too much subjectivity.

A crucial element of control is created by calling upon the judge to have what Jennifer Nedelsky calls an 'enlarged mentality', that is an active vision that enables him or her to rise above individual idiosyncracy to cover the standpoint of others belonging to the community to be persuaded. This calls for choosing judges from the ranks of those who have the experience and have demonstrated the capacity to function with such enlarged mentality. A second disciplining factor I have already mentioned is that in a multi-member court a number of different judges do the evaluations, so that individual personal preferences or prejudices tend to counteract each other. Finally, in the case of a judicial determination, there is the knowledge that judgments are communicated in public and their reasoning and internal coherence will be subjected to regular analysis and criticism by members of the broad legal community, as well as by the public.

It is important to recognize that the legal community does not consist only of members of the legal profession. It is a notional community, made up by all those who feel they are wearing legal hats when dealing with a problem. When I prepare a judgment I semi-consciously have in mind the full reach of this community. I think of all the people who might read it and be influenced by it. I search for the form of argument that I hope will convince them that I am on the right track, or, at the very least, that I am offering a plausible and defensible way of looking at the issue. This does not mean that I would say that my judgment is correct and that those who differ are wrong. There is a modesty inherent in the judicial function that prevents me from being convinced that I necessarily am right, or, rather, that there is only one right answer to a legal problem, and that it so happens that I am the one who has arrived at it. It has nothing to do with being personally humble; if you cannot be brazen when called upon to defend a position you truly believe in, you should not be on the Bench. My modesty is institutional, not personal. As a judge, I do not feel that it is our function actually to be right. Indeed, how can we all be right when we differ so much amongst ourselves? In my view, our duty in each case is to make our best efforts to be right. We give it our best shot, knowing that our judgments will enter the lists and engage with endless other judgments, many still to be written, in the timeless tournament of competing and converging legal ideas.

I have tried hard to imagine myself as Hercules, the figure playfully conjured up by Ronald Dworkin to suggest the judge who heroically refuses to be led into judicial temptation, rejects false arguments and arrives at the one correct answer that, theoretically, each legal problem should have. I realize that he is making a philosophical point, challenging the post-modernists who deny the very notion that there can be a right answer, as well as the super-realists who say we would be better off acknowledging that, however we may tart up the language, in reality we are simply using judicial power to express our personal prejudices or the dominant prejudices of our time. Yet I feel far more comfortable with the less exalting idea that all I am doing is using the tools of the law as I understand them, trying my best in a particular context at a particular moment to deal honestly and openly with the issues before me. I try to make my voice as legally clear, true and harmonious as possible. But I cannot help but see it as one voice among many. The fact that it will have consequences does not make it right. To my mind, the objective of the judge is not to pronounce the one and only correct answer to the question at issue. It is to contribute an honest voice to the ceaseless striving for the best expression of the law in relation to a particular case at a particular moment. And the criteria I use are those that have been legitimated by the thinking and practice of the legal community to which my judgment will be addressed.

To the extent that the community's understanding of the law needs constantly to evolve, I might be aware that a particular position I am advancing could be ahead of what most members of that community would regard as correct. Nevertheless I will put my name to it because my judicial conscience tells me that the need for change has ripened and that the new approach has to be legitimated to the extent that my judgment can purport to do so. My voice is just one that will enter the discourse, whether in harmony or in discord with all the other voices. If pure legal reasoning was all that was involved, it would be correct to speak about there possibly being only one right answer to a question. But to the extent that the exercise of judgment is at the heart of the project, I prefer to think that what is at stake is not the achievement of certainty for all time, but the accomplishment of maximum persuasiveness at that moment. Thus, I do not think it helpful to characterize the famous dissent by Oliver Wendell Holmes on freedom of speech as having been right at the time of its delivery. Nor do I feel it only became right when it later secured majority support. The same would apply to the great dissents of Brandeis. They represented important views articulating coherent legal philosophy at the time of their pronouncement. The lonely voice eventually became the dominant voice. That is the nature of the legal dialectic, and the hope that animates every person who writes a dissent.

So when I follow my legal conscience and articulate a judgment in a particular way, I think immediately of my colleagues on the Court who will be reading it, and console myself with the thought that if I do not persuade them this time round, perhaps I am planting the seed of a new approach by them in future cases. I imagine judges and magistrates in other courts, wrestling with their own judgments, reading it and possibly getting assistance from it. I think of legal practitioners pouncing on it in search of arguments to assist their clients. Having been a law teacher for many years, I envisage academics propelling their critical ploughs through it, discussing it with their students, and possibly using it as a footnote in their textbooks. And especially I think of students engaging with it, their minds still questing, their idealism alive. What can the law do for ordinary people? What language should the law use to express itself in accessible and persuasive form?

Then there is another class entirely of potential readers: members of Government who might have been involved in the case and who might have special responsibilities in the area being covered. I recall a Canadian Supreme Court judge telling me that the starting point for much judicial reasoning in the United States was that government was the foe, hence their declaration that the most fundamental of all rights was the right to be left alone. In Canada, he said, the courts saw government not as foe but as friend with whom the courts engaged in a joint enterprise to secure the rights and well-being of the people. I believe that, as in Canada, the South African Constitution envisages the legislature, the executive and the judiciary as all being involved in a common constitutionally-defined project to improve the lives of the people and protect human dignity, equality and freedom. The separation of powers acknowledges that in this regard each branch of government has special responsibilities while being subject to specific forms of public accountability. But the underlying assumption is that there will be civilized conversation rather than rude discourse between the three branches. There might be times when the judiciary feels that the particular way in which the Constitution has been violated calls for appropriately pointed language. But while ever-vigilant to take a stand against abuses of power, the courts should at the same time never lose sight of the difficult choices that the government has to make, the more so in a country where the need for transformation is great and the resources available for achieving it are relatively limited.

Civility in public life goes well beyond good manners. It is an element that favours democratic pluralism (see the *Masethla* case, at p 154). Accordingly, civility is explicitly required in the relations between the three branches of government themselves. Indeed, a dialogic relation between judiciary and government is inherent to the very structure of our Constitution. Our Court has extensive powers of judicial review, including the competence to declare an Act of Parliament invalid to the extent that it is inconsistent with the Constitution. This means that we are constantly dealing with challenges to the validity of legislation. The powers granted to our Court in this respect are great. When declaring a statute to be unconstitutional and invalid, we may make any order that is just and equitable, including one giving Parliament a grace period within which to correct the defect in the law. The notion of a dialogue or conversation with Parliament is therefore built into the very determination of our jurisdiction. And in my more vain moments I imagine that when they are considering how to draft a new law, members of Parliament will read what Sachs J had to say on a particular problem, or at least that their law advisors will glance at selected passages or summaries.

Then, of course, there is the Press. The media pick up on our judgments and communicate aspects to the public at large. To facilitate media understanding of what are often complicated and long judgments, the Court issues brief media summaries that outline the main issues and conclusions. Our aspiration is that the general public should become knowledgeable about their fundamental rights and understand the way in which government works. Our judgments could be major sources of such knowledge and understanding. The meaning of a judgment could go well beyond the determination of a dispute between particular parties. Court decisions help to create the basic value system of society and establish the character of our constitutional democracy. And every detail matters. Each judgment we write has to respect its public significance in every single part—as Mies van der Rohe said of his buildings, God is in the detail. One cannot be precise and accurate enough.

Moreover, however reduced the actual readership of any judgment of mine might be, its potential readership is vast. And merely being cognizant of this potential for extensive and diverse scrutiny acts as a strong warning against mental laziness. The objective is not to please or displease anyone, but to converse with as much rigour, integrity, and awareness of our constitutional responsibilities as possible, with as wide an audience as can be imagined. And my experience suggests that when it comes to decisions concerning fundamental rights, the language and concepts that appeal most strongly to the most highly trained members of the legal community are exactly those that register most positively with the lay public.

The legal community, of course, is not a clearly defined and stable entity. Problems of establishing commonalities will arise when the legal community is seen to be too enclosed and self-referential. Standards that may at any stage appear to leading members of the community to be neutral and incontestable, will be challenged by others who feel that in reality they embody prejudices that are all the more pernicious for being hidden and regarded as axiomatic. Thus feminist jurisprudence has long charged that the 'reasonable man' standard, so widely employed in the law, frequently has had an unconscious bias towards norms based on what men in our society would regard as part of the natural order of things. Feminists have declared that more was required than just a change in terminology from the 'reasonable man' to the 'reasonable person'. For example, courts should take account of the actual life experiences of women when considering the force that battered women could reasonably use to break out of debilitating terror produced by repeated violence; or refuse to treat pregnancy as though it were an illness: or put themselves in the shoes of a subordinate woman employee when deciding whether repeated banter with sexual innuendo constituted sexual harassment.

Similarly, supporters of using law as an instrument for protecting the environment had to overcome considerable resistance when seeking to alter legal points of reference that had long and tenaciously been adhered to by members of the established legal community. Thus a completely new legal vision had to be developed. It moved over decades from imagined ideals to soft law, and eventually to hard law. And it developed over time hitherto unfamiliar notions of fiduciary responsibility in favour of unborn generations; of legal protection extending beyond state boundaries; of the invocation of precautionary principles rather than negligence as the standard to be applied; and of giving to persons whose direct interests were not being threatened, the right to bring legal proceedings. The legal community cannot thus be seen as a fixed body of people bound by unchanging commonalities of thought. The norms and standards that define it are constantly being contested and ever-evolving. And like it or not, the judiciary will always find itself at the heart of this process, whether keeping pace with it, speeding it up or holding it back.

The question of who determines the standards has come to have particular relevance in a multi-cultural, multi-faith society like South Africa. The legal community was by law and in practice not only overwhelmingly white, but in addition, presumptively Christian, actively and unselfconsciously applying Christian standards as the norm for the whole of society. Thus, when all overtly racist statutes were repealed, we were still left with laws that gave a special place to certain Christian precepts.

Our Constitution is manifestly respectful of religious belief. Perhaps seventy percent of the population would call themselves Christian. People like Archbishop Desmond Tutu have played a most important role in public life. Our constitutional arrangements presuppose cooperation rather than strict separation between faith bodies and the state. Yet the Constitution resolutely protects the right to hold beliefs that are not theistic, and firmly turns its back on favouring one set of beliefs over another.

The result was that when preparing a judgment in a case involving the constitutionality of a prohibition against the sale of liquor on Sundays, Good Friday, and Christmas, I found it necessary to grapple with the question of whose standpoint should be used for purposes of evaluation. Should it be that of the reasonable Christian? Or the reasonable non-Christian? Or the reasonable non-believer? And what degree of sensitivity should be countenanced, that of the thick-skinned person, or the easily-wounded one? I eventually suggested that the reasonable person could be of any faith or no faith at all, and that he or she should be neither thick-skinned nor thin-skinned, but deeply sensitive to the values of our Constitution, including the right to equality and the right to live in an open and democratic society in which no particular world view would be prescribed by the state. The formulation appears in the *Lawrence* case (see p 156)—and I mention that it was not bath-induced, but the result of conscious and carefully thought-through reasoning (and it has not travelled).

In another case the issue was whether a Muslim widow would qualify as a surviving spouse for purposes of a right to seek maintenance from the estate of the man to whom she had been married according to Muslim law. Until the advent of our Constitution, South African courts had refused to treat Muslim and Hindu unions as marriages, because contrary to the way that marriage was 'understood in Christendom', they were not based on the union of one man and one woman for life, but were potentially polygamous. Writing for the majority of the Court, I stated that the linguistic appropriation of the word 'spouse' by a particular faith was no longer compatible with the notions of equality in our new Constitution (see the *Daniels* case, at p 159).

The legal community is by its nature both conservative in thinking, yet restless for change. Hence the dilemma facing a judge of deciding whether to locate him or herself as the upholder or the transformer of established legal principles. A principled judgment cannot, however, be based simply on a personal preference as to whether to move forward or stay still. Whether adhering to the status quo or supporting transformation, each judgment must be reasoned and justified in terms that the legal community would find at least defensible, if not totally convincing. In particular, a judgment that bases itself on introducing radical changes to the principles and standards hitherto firmly accepted by the legal community would have to set out persuasive references to the impact the new constitutional order has on re-defining the way the problem has to be looked at. Indeed, part of the extraordinary intensity of being a judge on the Constitutional Court has flowed from the knowledge that as a new court applying a new constitution it had constantly to be re-defining the norms and standards of judicial reasoning. Furthermore, it had to do so in a way that simultaneously destabilized the legal community by introducing change, and reinforced the community's self-assurance by justifying in a principled way the forward movement. In this regard I believe it is particularly important that when we re-arrange elements that the legal community has long regarded as virtually axiomatic, we explain precisely what we are doing in the most open and transparent way possible.

The *Masethla* Case

Civility as a constitutional requirement. In a case dealing with the manner in which the then President effectively and abruptly sacked the head of the National Intelligence Agency, I wrote in a separate concurring judgment about civility as a constitutional requirement.

SACHS J:

Fairness to an incumbent about to be relieved of a high profile position in public life presupposes the display of appropriate concern for the reputational consequences. People live not by bread alone; indeed in the case of career functionaries, reputation and bread are often inseparable. [And it] was not only the material benefits and the standing of the incumbent that had to be considered. The general public too had an interest. Constitutionally-created institutions need constantly to be nurtured if they are to function well. This requires that those who exercise public power should avoid wherever possible acting in a manner which may unduly disturb public confidence in the integrity of the incumbents of these institutions.

[F]air dealing and civility cannot be separated. Civility in a constitutional sense involves more than just courtesy or good manners. It is one of the binding elements of a constitutional democracy. It presupposes tolerance for those with whom one disagrees and respect for the dignity of those with whom one is in dispute. Civility, closely linked to ubuntu-botho, is deeply rooted in traditional culture, and has been widely supported as a precondition for the good functioning of contemporary democratic societies. Indeed, it was civilized dialogue in extremely difficult conditions that was the foundation of our peaceful constitutional revolution. The Constitution that emerged therefore presupposes that public power will be exercised in a manner that is not arbitrary and not unduly disrespectful of the dignity of those adversely affected by the exercise.

The *Lawrence* Case

When deciding whether a ban on the sale of liquor on Sundays, Christmas and Good Friday violated the right to freedom of religion, four members of the Court felt that freedom of religion was not infringed. Three others held that it was violated because the religious holidays of Christianity alone were being respected. My mind was eventually made up in a most unusual way: by seeing a hurt look on the face of my law clerk, Fatima. When I asked her what the frown was about, she pointed out that what appeared to be trivial could be deeply injurious when it formed part of a wider pattern of exclusion. So I wrote a separate judgment, supported by a colleague, holding that the state was indeed limiting religious freedom by endorsing a particular religion, however trifling the endorsement might seem. On the facts of the case, however, I held that the limitation was justifiable for achieving the meritorious secular objective of cutting down on alcohol abuse on double days of rest.

SACHS J:

What comes through as an innocuous part of daily living to one person who happens to inhabit a particular intellectual and spiritual universe, might be communicated as oppressive and exclusionary to another who lives in a different realm of belief. What may be so trifling in the eyes of members of the majority or a dominant section of the population as to be invisible, may assume quite large proportions and be eminently real, hurtful and oppressive to those upon whom it impacts. This will especially be the case when what is apparently harmless is experienced by members of the affected group as symptomatic of a wide and pervasive pattern of marginalisation and disadvantage.

In testing whether in the present case the State endorsed a particular set of beliefs in a manner which violated the right of religious freedom, I shall attempt to apply the sensibilities and perspectives neither of what has been called the 'reasonable Christian' nor, for example, of the reasonable Jew, Muslim, or Hindu, nor of the reasonable atheist, but of the reasonable South African (of any faith or of none) who is neither hypersensitive nor overly insensitive to the belief in question, but highly attuned to the requirements of the Constitution. In my opinion, such a reasonable South African is a person of common sense immersed in the cultural realities of our country and aware of the amplitude and nuanced nature of our Constitution. He or she neither attempts relentlessly to purge public life of even the faintest association with religion for fear of otherwise descending the slippery slope to theocracy, nor at the other extreme, regards the religiously-based practices of the past to be as natural and non-sectarian as the air one breathes simply because of their widespread acceptance.

Such...persons, in, my view would have little difficulty in accepting that whatever may be the deep and continuing special significance for Christians, the survival of Sunday, Good Friday and Christmas Day as secularised public holidays integrated into the programmes of rest, travel and, in the case of Christmas Day, festivity, of all South Africans, no longer represents State endorsement of religion. At the same time, however, they would have equally few doubts that the choice of these days as closed days for the purposes of the sale of liquor, and not to establish a common day of rest, does indicate a maintenance of pre-constitutional sectarian bias.

[*Note: The judgment went on to hold that although the prohibition limited the right to religious freedom of non-Christians, nevertheless the limitation was so slight and indirect, and the public benefit of limiting the intake of liquor on weekends and double holidays so potentially great, that, applying proportionality analysis, it could be justified in an open and democratic society. The result was that the prohibition was sustained on different grounds by five of the nine judges who heard the matter. A few weeks after the judgment was delivered, unthinkingly I went one Sunday to buy beer at a local supermarket only to discover that because of a ruling by the Constitutional Court, it could not be sold on that day!*]

The *Daniels* Case

Should a Muslim widow be regarded as a 'spouse' for the purposes of claiming maintenance under the Surviving Spouse Maintenance Act? I answered the question affirmatively, overturning a long line of decisions by South African courts in the colonial and apartheid era that women married by Muslim rites were akin to concubines and did not qualify as legally married spouses. A minority judgment agreed that Muslim wives were being unfairly discriminated against, but said the remedy lay not in interpreting the word 'spouse' in the way I did, but in declaring the section to be unconstitutional and reading in the words 'or married by Muslim or Hindu rites' to cure the defect.

SACHS J:

The word 'spouse' in its ordinary meaning includes parties to a Muslim marriage. Such a reading is not linguistically strained. On the contrary, it corresponds to the way the word is generally understood and used. It is far more awkward from a linguistic point of view to exclude parties to a Muslim marriage from the word 'spouse' than to include them. Such exclusion as was effected in the past did not flow from courts giving the word 'spouse' its ordinary meaning. Rather, it emanated from a linguistically strained use of the word flowing from a culturally and racially hegemonic appropriation of it. Such interpretation owed more to the artifice of prejudice than to the dictates of the English language. Both in intent and impact the restricted interpretation was discriminatory, expressly exalting a particular concept of marriage, flowing initially from a particular world-view, as the ideal against which Muslim marriages were measured and found to be wanting.

Discriminatory interpretations deeply injurious to those negatively affected were in the conditions of the time widely accepted in the courts. They are no longer sustainable in the light of our Constitution.

[As] Langa DP has stated:

> The Constitution is located in a history which involves a transition from a society based on division, injustice and exclusion from the democratic process to one which respects the dignity of all citizens, and includes all in the process of governance. As such, the process of interpreting the Constitution must recognize the context in which we find ourselves and the Constitution's goal of a society based on democratic values, social justice and fundamental human rights. This spirit of transition and transformation characterises the constitutional enterprise as a whole.... The Constitution requires that judicial officers read legislation, where possible, in ways which give effect to its fundamental values. Consistently with this, when the constitutionality of legislation is in issue, they are under a duty to examine the objects and purport of an Act and to read the provisions of the legislation, so far as is possible, in conformity with the Constitution.

In the present matter the constitutional values of equality, tolerance and respect for diversity point strongly in favour of giving the word 'spouse' a broad and inclusive construction, the more so when it corresponds with the ordinary meaning of the word.

7

The Judge Who Cried:
The Judicial Enforcement of
Socio-Economic Rights

The *Grootboom* Case

Mrs Grootboom decided she had had enough. She and her two children, and her sister with three children, lived in a shack in an area not far from Cape Town. The winter rains were approaching and she felt she could not bear another season in a waterlogged area. Altogether, about 5000 people lived in similar circumstances in the settlement, without clean water, or sewage or refuse removal services, and with virtually no electricity. Many had applied to the municipality for subsidized low-cost housing and had been on waiting lists for as long as seven years, with no relief in sight. Faced with the prospect of remaining indefinitely in intolerable conditions, Mrs Grootboom and nearly a thousand adults and children moved to a nearby vacant hill-side. The land had in fact been set aside for low-cost housing. Negotiations with the owner and the local council followed, but without success. Eventually a court order was issued declaring them to be in unlawful occupation of the land and requiring them to be evicted. They were then forcibly removed, prematurely and inhumanely, at the expense of the municipality. Their makeshift homes were bulldozed and burnt and their possessions destroyed. Many of the residents were not even present to salvage their meagre belongings.

Desperate and homeless, they moved onto a local dusty sports ground. Bitter Cape winter rains were arriving and they had little more than plastic sheeting for protection. They approached an attorney who wrote to the council describing the intolerable conditions under which they were living and demanded that the council meet its constitutional obligations and provide them with temporary accommodation. Dissatisfied with the municipality's response, the group launched an urgent application in the High Court. And so Mrs Grootboom gave her name to what came to be a highly-publicized case at the cutting-edge of world jurisprudence.

I imagined her (and the billions in the world like her) lying on the bare field at night staring up at the stars as the rainclouds gathered and asking: why are we born to live like this, why must my children grow up without a home? This was the query/challenge that lay under the more formal legal question: can social and economic rights be regarded as fundamental rights enforceable directly by the courts, and if so, how? Nearly all modern states have legislation that the courts enforce concerning housing, health, education and welfare. The issue was whether a right to housing flowed directly from the Constitution and as such had binding and overriding legal force in relation to legislation and policy on housing. And I thought back to the promise we had made in the years of struggle that the ending of apartheid would give the poor not only the right to vote, but the right to education, health and housing.

The South African Constitution in fact declared that everyone had the right to have access to adequate housing and that the state had to take reasonable legislative and other measures within its available resources, to achieve the progressive realisation of this right. What did these words mean for Mrs Grootboom?

The High Court ordered the municipality to provide temporary shelter pending the outcome of the application, so that it would not be compelled to determine the difficult and important questions under pressure of approaching rains. At the hearing the state acknowledged the dire circumstances in which the applicants found themselves. It contended, however, that these were the inherited consequences of past injustice, and not indications of a failure to meet current constitutional obligations. On the contrary, it argued, it was meeting these obligations by means of implementing a massive housing programme which enabled millions of poor people to move from leaking and makeshift shacks without secure tenure, to weatherproof homes to which they had full title. Three quarters of a million families had already been able to move into completely subsidized homes, serviced with electricity and water, and millions more would benefit in future as the housing programme unrolled.

The High Court accepted that the state in fact was meeting its obligation progressively to realise the right of access to adequate housing. The Court went on to hold, however, that the state had failed to meet a further and special obligation, namely, that which flowed from the rights of the child spelt out in the Constitution. The Court pointed out that the child's right to shelter was not qualified by reference to progressive realisation within available resources. The shelter envisaged by the section on children's rights might be less than adequate housing, but at the very least the state had an obligation to provide some protection from the elements. Furthermore, since the children could not be separated from their parents, the Court ordered that all the people concerned should be given at least elementary protection.

The state took the case on appeal to the Constitutional Court. I might mention that we were helped at the hearing in a most considerable way by the participation of the Human Rights Commission and the Community Law Centre of the University of the Western Cape. Counsel for the Legal Resources Centre appeared on their behalf and succeeded in broadening the debate so as to require the Court to consider the rights of all South Africans to shelter, whether they had children or not. The case showed the extent to which creative lawyers and energetic civil society organizations can help the poor to secure their basic rights.

How did the provision dealing with the right of access to adequate housing come to be in the Constitution? And the same question may be asked of similar provisions in the Bill of Rights dealing with access to health care, food, water and social security. How did they all come to be placed in the Constitution as fundamental rights which the state was obliged to realise progressively within its available resources? The existence of this large cluster of social and economic rights in the Bill of Rights added to the task facing our Court. We realised that in determining the scope of the right of access to adequate housing we would not only be resolving the case of Mrs Grootboom and others, we would also start exploring the whole question of the status of socio-economic rights in our Constitution, and more particularly, the extent of the state's constitutional duty when responding to claims for housing, health-care, food, water, and social security.

Origins of Enforceable Social and Economic Rights

My own direct confrontation with the question started in the mid-1980s when I was a law professor in exile in Mozambique. A group of black law students at the University of Natal-Durban established a body called the Anti-Bill of Rights Committee. I was shocked: What?!? Not Anti-Apartheid, but Anti-Bill of Rights!!! I was jolted by the notion of idealistic persons belonging to the oppressed community, part of the struggle for a non-racial democracy, being opposed to the idea of a Bill of Rights. Yet I understood and sympathized with much of their motivation. Some called it 'A Bill of Whites', seeing it as a document established in advance by a privileged white minority to block any future moves towards social and economic transformation. Their fear was that the Bill of Rights would defend the unjust socio-economic situation created by apartheid, guarantee property rights in terms of which whites owned 87% of the land and 95% of productive capital, and impose extreme limits on the capacity of the democratic state to equalize access to wealth. Ultimately, the poor would remain poor, albeit formally liberated, and the rich would get richer, though technically not advantaged.

Yet a number of forward-looking white judges and academics had advanced the need for a Bill of Rights precisely because they thought it would facilitate the achievement of majority rule. Their reasoning had been that while everyone would have the vote, and discrimination would be outlawed, a Bill of Rights would re-assure whites that they had a protected future in the country. The dialectic of legal development was such, however, that concepts intended to assuage the anxieties of the whites inevitably aroused the concerns of the blacks.

I was determined to keep this dialectic of estrangement from congealing in polarized form. I remember the time well. It was shortly before I was nearly killed by the bomb planted in my car in Mozambique by South African security agents. I wrote a paper for the Constitutional Committee of the ANC espousing the need to set up an 'Anti-Anti-Bill of Rights Committee'. The paper pointed out that every revolution was impossible until it happened, then it became inevitable, and in this unstable context we had to consider a future Bill of Rights for South Africa. The notion that the law students had of a Bill of Rights was unduly narrow, presupposing that the function of such a document was simply to limit the power of government to effect change. Yet there was no reason why a Bill of Rights should not also be an instrument for advancing the claims of the dispossessed. And at this point I introduced into the discourse the theme of the three generations of rights.

The first generation encompassed the classic civil and political rights which emerged from the French and American Revolutions. These were the fundamental rights of citizens as free persons, and they had to be spelt out unequivocally in any post-liberation document.

The second generation of rights dealt with entitlements concerning housing, health, education and welfare. They were introduced in France after the 1848 Revolution and Germany under Bismarck in the late 19th Century. Later they were taken up in the Russian Revolution and then came to be central to national policy in the so-called welfare states of the 20th Century. So they were developed in revolutionary, authoritarian, and social democratic countries. During World War II Roosevelt included 'freedom from want' in his four freedoms. After the War these rights gained strong international support and were integrated with civil and political rights into the Universal Declaration of Human Rights. They were subsequently entrenched in the International Covenant on Economic, Social and Cultural Rights, which, though adopted separately from the International Covenant on Civil and Political Rights, enjoyed equal legal status.

The concept of a third generation of rights, and, indeed, the whole notion of clustering rights in generational terms, was developed in the late 1970s by a Czech lawyer working at the United Nations. His concern was primarily with the right to a clean and healthy environment, a collective right which he could not fit easily into any known category of basic human rights. Hence he coined the idea of a third generation of rights, which by its nature would belong to the whole community and to future generations, and not just to individuals. Other similar rights, sometimes referred to as solidarity rights, were the right to development and the right to peace. My friend Kader Asmal referred to the three generation of rights as: 'blue rights' (civil and political); 'red rights' (socio-economic); and 'green rights' (human solidarity).

So the theme of social and economic rights was on the agenda. And when political prisoners were released in South Africa, and exiles like myself could go home, and when serious negotiations about a new constitutional order began, the debate moved to a new plane: that of enforceability. Three distinct positions emerged. There were those who argued that such rights should be seen as aspirational only, and not be embodied in any way in the constitution. A second current favoured incorporating such rights in the constitution, but giving them the status of guiding principles only and not making them enforceable by the courts. The third position was that appropriate language should be found to make them justiciable as enforceable constitutional rights.

The only precedents we could find pointed towards the midway position, that is, to incorporate socio-economic rights in the constitution merely as non-justiciable directives of state policy. Thus when the Irish achieved independence from Britain they included socio-economic rights in their Constitution but made it clear that such rights would not be enforceable by the courts. Similarly, when India won its independence after World War II, its Constituent Assembly adopted a constitution which included socio-economic rights simply as directives of state policy, stating in terms that they were not to be enforceable by the courts. (I mention in passing that the Indian Supreme Court went on to interpret these rights in a creative way, using them to give texture and substance to fundamental civil and political rights that were directly enforceable in the courts.) In the South African debate there was strong support for one separate chapter in the constitution to deal with rights that were to be enforceable, while another separate chapter would contain directives of state policy that would not be justiciable, that is they would not be directly enforceable in a court, but would merely serve as a guide for state policy.

It was at about this time, in the early 1990s, that I had the pleasure of being invited to spend a week in Paris as a guest of Robert Badinter, President of the French Conseil Constitutionel. Ronald Dworkin with whom I had worked when he had helped promote dialogue between South African judges and ANC lawyers in exile, happened to be in Paris. I was hoping to receive his comments on the Draft Bill of Rights produced by the ANC Constitutional Committee, and in particular on its provisions concerning the enforcement of socio-economic rights. We had an amusing telephone conversation. 'Where are you staying?' he asked. 'At the Palais Royale', I answered, 'not the Palais Royale Hotel, but the Palais Royale!' The Conseil in fact occupied the Palais and I was being accommodated in an apartment in the building. This gave me the bait for a meeting: would Ronald like to see the original copy of the Declaration of the Rights of Man? After the meeting, as we descended the steps of the Palais, he indicated his doubts about our draft Bill of Rights. Was it appropriate to include extensive and detailed social and economic rights as fundamental rights in a constitution? In his view, equal protection was a most powerful and principled instrument that could be used to strengthen the position of disadvantaged persons who had been forced by racial discrimination to live in conditions of gross inequality.

I spent much time pondering over his words. My conclusion, however, was that equal protection would not be enough, even when coupled with affirmative action. The problem was not simply to prevent continuing or new discrimination, but to ensure that everyone was entitled to at least the minimum decencies of life. Equal protection coupled with affirmative action would greatly assist the emerging new black middle class. But it would be far less helpful for the desperately poor. As it turned out, the equality clause came to occupy a central role in our new Bill of Rights. Yet, the equality provisions did not go beyond prohibiting negative discriminatory conduct and facilitating ameliorative action to redress patterns of disadvantage. It did not in itself require positive action on the part of the state to enable people to live in conditions consistent with at least the minimum standards of human dignity. In a country where a great section of the people lived in desperate poverty, affirmative action would not be enough; some form of broad social advancement was required. The question remained: should the obligation on the state to promote socio-economic advance be made a constitutional duty?

In Chapter Eight I write about problems created when unelected judges are empowered to decide social and economic questions normally within the purview of the elected branches of government. I conclude that when it comes to protecting the rights of marginalized and vulnerable groups, it may well be an advantage that our judges are not elected. In my opinion, however, the greatest problem concerning judicial enforcement of social and economic rights was not one of institutional illegitimacy. The real difficulty was that of institutional incapacity. A major objection to judges enforcing social and economic rights was that judges were likely to get it all wrong. This was because of the social class from which judges traditionally had been drawn, and the nature of traditional legal thinking, which tended to look at questions in abstract and formulaic ways that ignored the real lives of real people and ended up favouring the status quo. Parliament was there to deal with the practicalities of housing, land, and other social questions. It had hearings and received inputs from a variety of people with specialized expertise. Moreover, the very nature of the political process called for compromise and a balancing out of interests. In open and democratic society, political compromise based on the principle of give-and-take rather than the idea that winner-takes-all, was to be applauded. Yet judges were institutionally completely unsuited to take decisions on houses, hospitals, schools, and electricity. They just did not have the know-how and the capacity to handle those questions. But judges did know about human dignity, about oppression and about things that reduced a human being to a status below that which a democratic society would regard as tolerable. Efficiency may well be one of the great principles of government, and the utilitarian principle of producing the greatest good for the greatest number might well be the starting-off point for all uses of public resources. But the qualitative element, based on respect for the dignity of each and every one of us, should never be left out. This is where the vision of the judiciary, institutionally tunnelled in the direction of respect for human dignity, comes into its own. And the principled balancing that courts do is quite different from the compromises worked out in political life.

I suspect that behind the technical arguments advanced against the judicial enforcement of socio-economic rights, lay a basic concern that the involvement of the courts in this area would lead to a dilution of their respect for fundamental civil and political rights. Put crudely, there was a fear that in pursuit of the right to bread, the right to freedom would be submerged. Anxiety on this score had strong and unfortunate historical underpinning. Certain states had contended that in order to achieve national development and to improve the conditions of the impoverished masses, they had had to suppress freedom of speech, do away with multi-party democracy and spurn an open society. Could it be, though, that people wanted freedom without bread, or bread without freedom? In South Africa the struggle for the vote and for freedom of movement and speech, had always been inseparable from the fight for housing, health, and education. Bureaucratic authoritarianism had been intrinsic to apartheid; people simply did not count as human beings, hence the squalid housing and inferior education for the majority. The restoration of dignity for all South Africans accordingly required both the development of increased respect for the personality rights and freedom of each one of us and the creation of material conditions for a dignified life for all.

Our experience in fact demonstrates that instead of undermining each other, freedom and bread were interrelated and interdependent. As Amartya Sen has shown, in open and democratic societies you do not see famine, because shortages of food are dealt with in ways in which there is public accountability for distribution. In dictatorships, on the other hand, despite the same quantity of food being available you will find famine and starvation because grain is secretly hoarded and siphoned off to the rich. It heaps indignity upon indignity to say that the poor are not interested in the franchise, or the right to speak their mind, or the right to be treated fairly, and that their only concern is with filling their stomachs. In general terms, the greatest sacrifices for freedom have been made by those who are the poorest and most dispossessed. The dignity for which they fought encompasses both the vote and a decent life. Where the struggle for survival is overwhelming, freedom to vote and the right to criticize the government risk becoming devoid of practical meaning. Yet the vote can be a tool for getting a better life, and conversely, in a society where the people are educated, where they can read and study and learn about the world, they can make informed political decisions and exercise meaningful individual choices. It would have been ironical indeed if the struggle had ended up doing little more than to guarantee to people dying of hunger the inalienable right to use their last breath freely to curse the government.

The inter-relatedness of the different generations of rights helps resolve some of the libertarian versus communitarian tensions inherent in the enforcement of social and economic rights. Libertarians focus on the individual and place great emphasis on autonomy and choice. Communitarians assert that we all live in communities and that our capacity to make and execute choices about our lives is largely dictated by the social setting in which we function. Applying an extreme libertarian approach to Mrs Grootboom's situation would have secured to her the right to be left alone, with unrestricted freedom to denounce the government as the rain pelted down on her. Yet she did not want the state to leave her alone. She wanted to be able to call upon the state to ensure that she and her children had a roof over their heads. On the other hand, if a radical communitarian approach had been adopted, the invasion by herself and a thousand others of privately-owned land could, without more, have been justified as asserting the rights of a large group of homeless people as against the rights of one landowner. The fact was, however, that apart from the rights of the landowner, there were other individuals in the queue for formal housing due to be built on that land, and their rights were also being affected.

In my opinion, the approach that our Constitution required us to adopt was neither a purely libertarian one, nor simply communitarian. It was dignitarian. Respect for human dignity united the right to be autonomous with the need to recognise that we all live in communities. It was the fundamental right of all human beings to have their basic human dignity respected, that linked the right to freedom with the right to bread.

The *Soobramoney* Case

Before I get to the manner in which the Court dealt with Mrs Grootboom's problem, I must mention that we had had one earlier case concerning the enforcement of socio-economic rights. It was an extremely poignant matter, brought to us by someone close to death. It dealt with the right of access to healthcare, and in particular to emergency medical treatment.

Mr Soobramoney, who was suffering from chronic renal failure and other heart and sugar-related problems, approached our Court asking us to order the state hospital's dialysis service to keep death away for as long as its machines could keep him alive. He had previously received a session of life-saving dialysis treatment at a state hospital, but had been told that he did not qualify for further treatment because resources permitted only thirty per cent of persons suffering from chronic renal failure to be treated. Priority was given to those who could benefit from renal transplants, and since he was a poor candidate for such transplants, he had to stay at the back of the queue. Mr Soobramoney had managed to survive for some time on dialysis in the private medical sector, but when his family's funds had run out, he had once more sought free treatment from a state hospital. On being turned away he went to court, claiming that his constitutional rights to access to health care services, and not to be refused emergency medical treatment, were being denied.

This was a most painful case. Effectively, it was up to the eleven men and women on the Court to decide whether this man lived or died. There was no precedent to guide us—all we had was the text of the Constitution, a hospital with good but limited resources, and the pleas of a dying man.

We decided first that his claim based on the right to emergency medical treatment had to be rejected. In our view, the right to emergency care could be claimed on behalf of someone who collapsed or was the victim of sudden trauma. It did not apply to chronic medical conditions, even if they had reached life-threatening proportions. If all chronic illnesses were to be regarded as emergency cases entitled to treatment at state expense, there would be no funds left in the public health budget for other pressing services such as mother and child care, health education, immunization, the prevention and treatment of diseases such as TB, cancer and malaria, and the amelioration of HIV/AIDS.

As far as the right of access to health care was concerned, the Court found that the access granted by the state health services to Mr Soobramoney had not been shown to be unreasonable. The evidence from the hospital indicated that their plan was eminently rational and non-discriminatory, and accordingly his claim on this ground failed as well. (See the *Soobramoney* case, at p 185.)

In the course of argument I said to counsel that I appreciated the dignity with which his client had approached the Court, and that if resources were co-existent with compassion, the case would have been easy to determine. And in a written judgment concurring with the main judgment, I pointed out that the problem in all cases concerned with enforcing socio-economic rights was precisely that resources were always limited. In this context I stated that social and economic rights by their very nature involved rationing. Such rationing should not be considered a restriction of the right of access to health care, but the very precondition for its proper exercise. Socio-economic rights in this respect were different in their mode of enjoyment, if not in their essence, from civil and political rights. The right to free speech was not by its nature rationed. Everybody could speak their mind just as everybody above a certain age could vote. Difficult problems may arise in terms of their practical exercise, for example in relation to access to public broadcasting or having the financial means to establish independent media or running an election campaign. But the rights are fully-fledged from the start, and not subject to progressive realization. The progressive realisation of socio-economic rights within available resources, on the other hand, indicates that a system of apportionment was fundamental to their very being. (See the *Soobramoney* case—broader questions, at p 188.)

I was not sure as to the full implications of this distinction, both in terms of conceptualizing the nature of the right and in respect of determining appropriate remedies for a breach. Yet I was convinced that the exercise of a right that by its nature is shared, often competitively, with other holders of the right, must have different legal characteristics from the exercise of a classical individual civil right that is autonomous and complete in itself.

The state was obliged to take measures progressively to realise the right of access to health care. Thus, the state could fulfil its duty in respect of providing such access as much by measures to provide safe water, clean air, and basic nutrition for the whole community, as by providing a place in a hospital and expensive curative treatment for an individual. What was important was that the reach of health programmes became progressively larger and that every individual had a right to be considered fairly and without discrimination for treatment within each programme.

Returning to the *Grootboom* Case

To return to Mrs Grootboom's case. Taking constitutional rights seriously calls for judicial sensitivity to risk two temptations. The one is to be unduly formalistic showing a passive and uncaring attitude to the real lives of actual people. The other is to be overly eager to secure favourable headlines as champions of the poor. I think all the judges in the *Grootboom* matter were aware of the need to avoid judicial populism, that is, to resist any desire to make orders that captured the popular imagination, but which would not be sustainable in practice. Yet our oath to do justice to all required us to give meaning and content to the socio-economic rights as set out in our Bill of Rights. The factual situation in which Mrs Grootboom and the others found themselves clamoured for some kind of response. The right of access to adequate housing would have no meaning if a thousand people, in this case as a result of state action, were left without a place to lay their heads and without even minimal shelter, only a spot on a dusty ground and a few pieces of protective plastic sheeting. The problem facing us then was how to find a secure jurisprudential foundation for responding to their situation, that is, how to provide a principled analysis and remedy that would be consonant with our limited institutional capacity, and yet be capable of meaningful enforcement.

In a unanimous judgment prepared by Justice Zak Yacoob, we held that the key concept in the provision on access to adequate housing was the obligation on the state to take 'reasonable legislative and other measures' progressively to realize the right. We felt that the concept of reasonable measures was one capable of being adjudicated on by our Court. If the measures failed to meet the standard of reasonableness then the state would be in breach of its constitutional obligations. In deciding whether the measure met this standard the Court would acknowledge the special expertise of the government in this area and accept the fact that a wide range of policy choices would be consistent with reasonableness. Yet, however impressive the state housing programme had been, it had failed to make provision for persons such as Mrs Grootboom who had found themselves in situations of such crisis and desperation that their dignity had been seriously assailed. In other words, though the programme was reasonable in its broad reach, it had one serious gap which prevented it from satisfying constitutional requirements. It contained no comprehensive plan to deal with homeless people in situations of extreme desperation, such as victims of disaster, or persons in Mrs Grootboom's situation. We accordingly declared the housing programme of the state to be unreasonable and in conflict with the Constitution to the extent that 'it failed to make reasonable provision within its available resources for people...with no access to land, no roof over their heads, and who were living in intolerable conditions or crisis situations'.

Having made that declaration, that is, having established the nature of the state's obligations in this area, we then left it to the state to decide how best in practice it could remedy its failure. Thus, we left it open to the state to decide whether the programme for emergency shelter should operate nationally, provincially or locally, and how the programme should best be developed; whether the programme would involve only providing dry land on which people could erect shelters, or whether it would provide both land and houses, or whether it would be more efficacious for the state to provide sufficient financial assistance for the affected persons to make their own housing arrangements. Similarly, we left it to the state to decide where it was to get the money for the emergency programme; it could take it from the formal housing programme, it could take it from defence, it could raise new taxes, it could take it from anywhere—except, I should add, from the judges' salaries, which were constitutionally protected!

It was in this way that we sought to express the need both to remind the state of its duty to protect the fundamental dignity of human beings, and to recognize the fact that it was the role of the government to determine the priorities, texture and detail of the manner in which it should fulfil its responsibilities.

In seeking to arrive at a principled determination capable of being operational and effective, we were strongly influenced by the need to deal with the rights set out in our Bill of Rights on the basis that they were interrelated and interdependent. Our Constitution says that in interpreting our Bill of Rights we must promote the values of human dignity, equality and freedom. It was respect for these values, and especially the value of human dignity, that guided us. We accordingly made it plain that the right of access to housing could not be separated from the right to human dignity. This meant that a purely quantitative response by the state to its obligations would not be enough, even if by international standards it made extraordinary provision for access to formal housing. The qualitative dimension could never be forgotten. (See the *Grootboom* case, at p 191.)

The *Treatment Action Campaign* Case

The next case concerning the enforcement of socio-economic rights was not long in coming, nor was it any less dramatic. It dealt with the right of access to health care in the context of the severe HIV/AIDS pandemic which had hit our country. In particular, it related to the right of pregnant women living with HIV to receive the drug Nevirapine in all state hospitals and clinics, and not only in two facilities in each of the nine provinces as provided for by the Department of Health. The drug substantially cut the transmission to the newborn baby of the virus, and the state policy was that its distribution should be limited pending evaluation for two years of the problems associated with its management.

The case, brought by the Treatment Action Campaign (TAC), described by its counsel as the most lively and effective civil society organization in South Africa, provoked emotion. The TAC had mobilized many tens of thousands of people living with HIV to refuse to see themselves as marginalized victims of a terrible disease, but rather to affirm themselves as people actively determining their lives as best they could. Some of the leaders had been in the struggle against apartheid, and knew how to combine street campaigning with use of the media and development of litigation. Their constitutional complaint was that the government was unreasonable and in default of its constitutional obligations to the extent that it was restricting the supply of Nevirapine to two sites only in each province. They pointed to the fact that the drug was being supplied by the manufacturers free for five years, and that its safety was not in issue because it could freely be bought over the counter by those who could pay. They produced evidence to show that doctors and nurses in medical facilities outside of the eighteen selected sites were eager to dispense it.

Counsel for the state argued forcefully, on the other hand, that the questions raised belonged to the sphere of government policy, and accordingly fell outside the domain of the judiciary. They put it bluntly: it was not for judges to prescribe drugs. In essence, the argument was based on the separation of powers doctrine, and if accepted, would to some extent have curtailed the scope of our decision in *Grootboom*.

I should add that counsel for the TAC contended that the decision in *Grootboom* did not go far enough. He argued that the Bill of Rights was based on the notion of individual rights. In his view, the Constitution required more from the judiciary than an insistence that the state design and implement reasonable programmes. It obliged the courts to come to the assistance of any individual whose life circumstances fell below the minimum core of entitlements consistent with the maintenance of human dignity.

I recall vividly an exchange between counsel and myself on this score. I put to him the following question: Did he mean that somebody living in the mountains can come to court and says he wants water from a tap, even if the money spent on meeting his particular claim could be used to furnish water for ten thousand people living lower down on the plains? That was an emotional argument, he replied. No, I suggested, it was part of promoting the best use of scarce resources to realize social and economic rights. And, I asked, should only those individuals with the sharpest elbows (and the best lawyers) get a house, water and electricity, and furthermore, should the Constitution be read as handing over to each judge in each court the right and duty to decide who should have priority access to social goods in short supply? Yes, he replied, if the individuals concerned were below the level of existence consistent with dignity, their rights were being infringed.

Possibly to the dismay of sectors of the human rights community, the Court eventually decided in effect that the minimum core obligation could be satisfied through broad governmental programmes aimed at meeting minimum needs, and did not have to be met by acknowledging individual entitlements enforceable in the courts. The impossibility of managing such individual claims through court proceedings would end up discrediting the notion of social and economic rights, and those most in need would end up even worse off.

From a public point of view, however, the main interest in the case lay in how our judgment would deal with the argument by counsel for the Minister of Health that, whatever our personal views might have been, it was constitutionally inappropriate for us as judges to determine health policies. In response to this separation of powers argument, the judges had asked counsel whether it was not the Constitution itself that had given the Court the task of enforcing constitutional rights. If so, would we not in fact be fulfilling our obligation in terms of the separation of powers doctrine when we used our judicial authority to ensure that the Constitution was respected?

As we were going into Court to deliver the judgment, my colleague Sandile Ngcobo playfully offered me a handkerchief and asked: 'Albie, will you need this today?' He was referring to a reaction of mine to an earlier judgment he had written for the

Court, and about which I had frequently spoken on my travels. It had concerned a person living with HIV who, having applied for a job as a steward on South African Airways aeroplanes, had passed all the entrance exams, but had been declared ineligible because of his HIV status. South African Airways had said, amongst other things, that British Airways did not employ people in his situation because it feared its customers might flee to a different airline. In his judgment, Sandile Ngcobo had firmly rejected the proposition that the commercial practices of other airlines could determine the constitutional rights of South Africans. The very fact that people were subject to prejudice, he had stated on behalf of the Court, was a reason for the airline to combat marginalization, not concede to it. He had therefore declared the applicant to be a victim of unfair discrimination and ordered South African Airways to employ him as a steward for as long as his health did not prevent him from serving customers properly. (See the *Hoffmann* case, at p 195.)

The courtroom had been packed with people wearing T-shirts saying 'HIV Positive'. There had been complete silence as we had handed down judgment. Then moments later when we had gone out to the passage at the back, I had heard cheering, and had found myself suddenly with tears in my eyes. It had not just been because of emotion about the impact of AIDS upon our country. The tears had come because of an overwhelming sense of pride at being a member of a court that protected fundamental rights and secured dignity for all. The emotion then had taken me unawares; now I felt emotionally prepared. So when we were about to enter the chamber to deliver judgment in the TAC case I said, 'No problem, Sandile. Today I'm ready, you can keep your hankie.'

As we filed into court I saw that again it was packed with people—young and old, men and women, black and white, the nation—wearing T-shirts marked 'HIV Positive'. There were also journalists from all over the world. The atmosphere was tense but the Court was completely still as Arthur Chaskalson, the Chief Justice, read out a summary of our decision in magisterial voice: since the drug was available without cost and was deemed safe enough for use in the private sector and in the test sites, limiting its supply on the ground that the government wanted to do further research on operational problems was not reasonable. It had to be borne in mind that large numbers of children would unnecessarily be born with HIV in the meantime, and that doctors had said clearly that they wanted to prescribe the drugs but were prevented from doing so by directives from the Ministry. The Court therefore declared that the drug should be made available to all state health facilities where the medical personnel in charge were able to manage their use for patients who had given informed consent. (See the *Treatment Action Campaign* case at p 198.) Once again, after the judgment was delivered there was total silence. We filed out of the court and stood together for a moment in the passage. Then, once more, cheering broke out. And, once again, I cried.

The *Soobramoney* Case

Mr Soobramoney, who was suffering from severe renal failure, asked the Court to order a state hospital to provide him with dialysis, stating that the Constitution guaranteed him the right of access to health care. The Court refused on the basis that it would not interfere with a rationally arrived at decision of the medical authorities on how best to use scarce resources, more particularly, to give preference to patients who would be good candidates for renal transplants. Arthur Chaskalson, then President of the Court and later Chief Justice, wrote for the Court.

CHASKALSON P:

We live in a society in which there are great disparities in wealth. Millions of people are living in deplorable conditions and in great poverty. There is a high level of unemployment, inadequate social security, and many do not have access to clean water or to adequate health services. These conditions already existed when the Constitution was adopted and a commitment to address them, and to transform our society into one in which there will be human dignity, freedom and equality, lies at the heart of our new constitutional order. For as long as these conditions continue to exist that aspiration will have a hollow ring...

By using the available dialysis machines in accordance with the guidelines more patients are benefited than would be the case if they were used to keep alive persons with chronic renal failure, and the outcome of the treatment is also likely to be more beneficial because it is directed to curing patients, and not simply to maintaining them in a chronically ill condition. It has not been suggested that these guidelines are unreasonable or that they were not applied fairly and rationally when the decision was taken by the Addington Hospital that the appellant did not qualify for dialysis...

The provincial administration which is responsible for health services in KwaZulu-Natal has to make decisions about the funding that should be made available for health care and how such funds should be spent. These choices involve difficult decisions to be taken at the political level in fixing the health budget, and at the functional level in deciding upon the priorities to be met. A court will be slow to interfere with rational decisions taken in good faith by the political organs and medical authorities whose responsibility it is to deal with such matters...

One cannot but have sympathy for the appellant and his family, who face the cruel dilemma of having to impoverish themselves in order to secure the treatment that the appellant seeks in order to prolong his life. The hard and unpalatable fact is that if the appellant were a wealthy man he would be able to procure such treatment from private sources; he is not and has to look to the state to provide him with the treatment. But the state's resources are limited and the appellant does not meet the criteria for admission to the renal dialysis programme. Unfortunately, this is true not only of the appellant but of many others who need access to renal dialysis units or to other health services. There are also those who need access to housing, food and water, employment opportunities, and social security. These are aspects of the right to '... human life: the right to live as a human being, to be part of a broader community to share in the experience of humanity.'...

The state has to manage its limited resources in order to address all these claims. There will be times when this requires it to adopt a holistic approach to the larger needs of society rather than to focus on the specific needs of particular individuals within society...

The *Soobramoney* Case—
Broader Questions

In a separate concurring judgment I dealt with some broader questions concerning the character of social and economic rights:

SACHS J:

While each claimant seeking access to public medical treatment is entitled to individualized consideration, the lack of principled criteria for regulating such access could be more open to challenge than the existence and application of such criteria. As a UNESCO publication put it: 'Even in the industrialized nations where public tax-supported research had made a private biomedical technology industry possible, the literal provision of equal access to high-technology care, utilized most often by the elderly, would inevitably raise the level of spending to a point which would preclude investment in preventive care for the young, and maintenance care for working adults. That is why most national health systems do not offer, or severely ration (under a variety of disguises), expensive technological care such as renal dialysis or organ transplants.' . . .

The inescapable fact is that if governments were unable to confer any benefit on any person unless it conferred an identical benefit on all, the only viable option would be to confer no benefit on anybody . . .

Health care rights by their very nature have to be considered not only in a traditional legal context structured around the ideas of human autonomy but in a new analytical framework based on the notion of human interdependence. A healthy life depends upon social interdependence: the quality of air, water, and sanitation which the state maintains for the public good; the quality of one's caring relationships, which are highly correlated to health; as well as the quality of health care and support furnished officially by medical institutions and provided informally by family, friend, and the community. As Minow puts it: 'Interdependence is not a social ideal, but an inescapable fact; the scarcity of resources forces it on us. Who gets to use dialysis equipment? Who goes to the front of the line for the kidney transplant?'...

Traditional rights analyses accordingly have to be adapted so as to take account of the special problems created by the need to provide a broad framework of constitutional principles governing the right of access to scarce resources and to adjudicate between competing rights bearers. When rights by their very nature are shared and interdependent, striking appropriate balances between the equally valid entitlements or expectations of a multitude of claimants should not be seen as imposing limits on those rights...

However the right to life may come to be defined in South Africa, there is in reality no meaningful way in which it can constitutionally be extended to encompass the right indefinitely to evade death. As Steven J puts it: dying is part of life, its completion rather than its opposite. We can, however, influence the manner in which we come to terms with our mortality. It is precisely here, where scarce artificial life prolonging resources have to be called upon, that tragic medical choices have to be made...

Courts are not the proper place to resolve the agonizing personal and medical problems that underlie these choices.

Important though our review functions are, there are areas where institutional incapacity and appropriate constitutional modesty require us to be especially cautious. Our country's legal system simply 'cannot replace the more intimate struggle that must be borne by the patient, those caring for the patient, and those who care about the patient'.

The provisions of the Bill of Rights should furthermore not be interpreted in a way which results in courts feeling themselves unduly pressurised by the fear of gambling with the lives of claimants into ordering hospitals to furnish the most expensive and improbable procedures, thereby diverting scarce medical resources and prejudicing the claims of others...

The applicant in this case presented his claim in a most dignified manner and showed manifest appreciation for the situation of the many other persons in the same harsh circumstances as himself. If resources were co-extensive with compassion, I have no doubt as to what my decision would have been. Unfortunately, the resources are limited, and I can find no reason to interfere with the allocation undertaken by those better equipped than I to deal with the agonising choices that had to be made.

The *Grootboom* Case

The Court declared that although the state had developed a large-scale programme to enable people to move from shacks into formal housing, it was not reasonable for it not to produce a further programme to provide appropriate shelter for desperate people who had no roof at all over their heads because of eviction, fire or floods. In his judgment for a unanimous Court, Justice Zacariah Yacoob said the following:

YACOOB J:

Our Constitution entrenches both civil and political rights and social and economic rights. All the rights in our Bill of Rights are inter-related and mutually supporting. There can be no doubt that human dignity, freedom and equality, the fundamental values of our society, are denied those who have no food, clothing or shelter. Affording socio-economic rights to all people therefore enables them to enjoy the other rights enshrined in [the Bill of Rights]. The realization of these rights is also key to the advancement of race and gender equality and the evolution of a society in which men and women are equally able to achieve their full potential...

In this regard, there is a difference between the position of those who can afford to pay for housing, even if it is only basic though adequate housing, and those who cannot. For those who can afford to pay for adequate housing, the State's primary obligation lies in unlocking the system, providing access to housing stock and a legislative framework to facilitate self-built houses through planning laws and access to finance. Issues of development and social welfare are raised in respect of those who cannot afford to provide themselves with housing. State policy needs to address both these groups. The poor are particularly vulnerable and their needs require special attention...

The State's obligation to provide access to adequate housing depends on context, and may differ from province to province, from city to city, from rural to urban areas and from person to person. Some may need access to land and no more; some may need access to land and building materials; some may need access to finance; some may need access to services such as water, sewage, electricity and roads. What might be appropriate in a rural area where people live together in communities engaging in subsistence farming may not be appropriate in an urban area where people are looking for employment and a place to live...

Reasonableness must also be understood in the context of the Bill of Rights as a whole. The right of access to adequate housing is entrenched because we value human beings and want to ensure that they are afforded their basic human needs. A society must seek to ensure that the basic necessities of life are provided to all if it is to be a society based on human dignity, freedom and equality. To be reasonable, measures cannot leave out of account the degree and extent of the denial of the right they endeavour to realise. Those whose needs are the most urgent and whose ability to enjoy all rights therefore is most in peril, must not be ignored by the measures aimed at achieving realisation of the right. It may not be sufficient to meet the test of reasonableness to show that the measures are capable of achieving a statistical advance in the realisation of the right. Furthermore, the Constitution requires that everyone must be treated with care and concern. If the measures, though statistically successful, fail to respond to the needs of those most desperate, they may not pass the test...

There is no express provision to facilitate access to temporary relief for people who have no access to land, no roof over their heads, for people who are living in intolerable conditions and for people who are in crisis because of natural disasters such as floods and fires, or because their homes are under threat of demolition. These are people in desperate need. Their immediate need can be met by relief short of housing which fulfils the requisite standards of durability, habitability and stability encompassed by the definition of housing development in the Act...

What has been done in execution of this programme is a major achievement. Large sums of money have been spent and a significant number of houses has been built. Considerable thought, energy, resources and expertise have been and continue to be devoted to the process of effective housing delivery. It is a programme that is aimed at achieving the progressive realisation of the right of access to adequate housing. A question that nevertheless must be answered is whether the measures adopted are reasonable...

The proposition that rights are interrelated and are all equally important is not merely a theoretical postulate. The concept has immense human and practical significance in a society founded on human dignity, equality and freedom. It is fundamental to an evaluation of the reasonableness of state action that account be taken of the inherent dignity of human beings. The Constitution will be worth infinitely less than its paper if the reasonableness of state action concerned with housing is determined without regard to the fundamental constitutional value of human dignity. Section 26, read in the context of the Bill of Rights as a whole, must mean that the respondents have a right to reasonable action by the state in all circumstances and with particular regard to human dignity. In short, I emphasise that human beings are required to be treated as human beings...

The *Hoffmann* Case

South African Airways [SAA] refused to allow Mr Hoffmann, who was living with HIV, to work as a steward. The judgment by Sandile Ngcobo for a unanimous Court held that this constituted unfair discrimination and ordered that he be employed as a steward for as long as his health permitted.

NGCOBO J:

At the heart of the prohibition of unfair discrimination is the recognition that under our Constitution all human beings, regardless of their position in society, must be accorded equal dignity. That dignity is impaired when a person is unfairly discriminated against. The determining factor regarding the unfairness of the discrimination is its impact on the person discriminated against. Relevant considerations in this regard include the position of the victim of the discrimination in society, the purpose sought to be achieved by the discrimination, the extent to which the rights or interests of the victim of the discrimination have been affected and whether the discrimination has impaired the human dignity of the victim. . . .

The Appellant is living with HIV. People who are living with HIV constitute a minority. Society has responded to their plight with intense prejudice. They have been subjected to systemic disadvantage and discrimination. They have been stigmatized and marginalized. As the present case demonstrates, they have been denied employment because of their HIV positive status without regard to their ability to perform the duties of the position from which they have been excluded. Society's response to them has forced many of them not to reveal their HIV status for fear of prejudice. This in turn had deprived them of the help they would otherwise have received. People who are living with HIV/AIDS are one of the most vulnerable groups in our society. Notwithstanding the availability of compelling medical evidence as to how this disease is transmitted, the prejudices and stereotypes against HIV positive people still persist. In view of the prevailing prejudice against HIV positive people, any discrimination against them can, to my mind, be interpreted as a fresh instance of stigmatization and I consider this to be an assault on their dignity. The impact of discrimination on HIV positive people is devastating. It is even more so when it occurs in the context of employment. It denies them the right to earn a living. For this reason, they enjoy special protection in our law . . .

Legitimate commercial requirements are, of course, an important consideration in determining whether to employ an individual. However, we must guard against allowing stereotyping and prejudice to creep in under the guise of commercial interests. The greater interests of society require the recognition of the inherent dignity if every human being and the elimination of all forms of discrimination. It is only when these groups are protected that we can be sure that our own rights are protected . . . The constitutional right of the appellant not to be unfairly discriminated against cannot be determined by ill-informed public perception of persons with HIV. Nor can it be dictated by the policies of other airlines not subject to our Constitution . . .

Prejudice can never justify unfair discrimination. This country has recently emerged from institutionalized prejudice. Our law reports are replete with cases in which prejudice was taken into consideration in denying the rights that we now take for granted. Our constitutional democracy has ushered in a new era—it is an era characterized by respect for human dignity for all human beings. In this era, prejudice and stereotyping have no place. Indeed, if as a nation we are to achieve the goal of equality that we have fashioned in our Constitution we must never tolerate prejudice, either directly or indirectly. SAA, as a state organ, has a constitutional duty to uphold the Constitution and may not avoid its constitutional duty by bowing to prejudice and stereotyping...

People who are living with HIV must be treated with compassion and understanding. We must show *ubuntu* towards them. They must not be condemned to 'economic death' by the denial of equal opportunity to employment. This is particularly true in our country, where the incidence of HIV infection is said to be disturbingly high.

The *Treatment Action Campaign* Case

The Court unanimously decided that it was unreasonable for the Department of Health to restrict the supply of the anti-retroviral drug Nevirapine to only two sites in each of the Provinces for a two year trial period. It declared that it should be made immediately available to all mothers living with HIV and their newborn babies in all state facilities where doctors could manage the process. The judgment dealt with the question of the separation of powers between the executive and the judiciary, in the terms that follow.

THE COURT:

The state is obliged to take responsible measures progressively to eliminate or reduce the large areas of severe deprivation that afflict our society...It should be borne in mind that in dealing with such matters the courts are not institutionally equipped to make the wide-ranging factual and political enquiries necessary for determining what the minimum-core standards called for should be, nor for deciding how public revenues should most effectively be spent. There are many pressing demands on the public purse...Courts are ill-suited to adjudicate upon issues where court orders could have multiple social and economic consequences for the community. The Constitution contemplates rather a restrained and focused role for the courts, namely, to require the state to take measures to meet its constitutional obligations and to subject the reasonableness of these measures to evaluation. Such determination of reasonableness may in fact have budgetary implications, but are not in them-selves directed at rearranging budgets. In this way the judicial legislative and executive functions achieve appropriate consti-tutional balance...

We are also conscious of the daunting problems confronting government as a result of the pandemic. And besides the pan-demic, the state faces huge demands in relation to access to education, land, housing, health care, food, water and social security. These are the socio-economic rights entrenched in the Constitution, and the state is obliged to take reasonable legislative and other measures, within its available resources to achieve the progressive realization of each of them. In light of our history this is an extraordinarily difficult task. Nonetheless it is an obligation imposed on the state by the Constitution...

Counsel for the government contended that under the sep-aration of powers the making of policy is the prerogative of the executive and not the courts, and the courts cannot make orders that have the effect of requiring the executive to pursue a particular policy. The Court has made it clear on more than one occasion that although there are no bright lines that separate the roles of the legislature, the executive and the courts from one another, there are certain matters that are pre-eminently within the domain of one or other of the arms of government and not the others. All arms of government should be sensitive to and respect this separation. This does not mean, however, that courts cannot or should not make orders that have an impact on policy...

The primary duty of courts is to the Constitution and the law, 'which they must apply impartially and without fear, favour or prejudice'. The Constitution requires the state to 'respect, protect, promote, and fulfill the rights in the Bill of Rights'. Where state policy is challenged as inconsistent with the Constitution, courts have to consider whether in formulating and implementing such policy the state has given effect to its constitutional obligation. If it should hold in any given case that the state has failed to do so, it is obliged by the Constitution to say so. In so far as that constitutes an intrusion into the domain of the executive, that is an intrusion mandated by the Constitution itself. There is also no merit in the argument advanced on behalf of government that a distinction should be drawn between declaratory and mandatory orders against government. Even simple declaratory orders against government or organs of state can affect their policy and may well have budgetary implications. Government is constitutionally bound to give effect to such orders whether or not they affect its policy and has to find the resources to do so. Thus, in the *Mpumalanga* case, this Court set aside a provincial government's policy decision to terminate the payment of subsidies to certain schools and ordered that payments should continue for several months. Also, in the case of *August* the Court in order to afford prisoners the right to vote, directed the electoral Commission to alter its election policy, planning and regulations, with manifest cost implications...

The magnitude of the HIV/AIDS challenge facing the country calls for a concerted, co-ordinated and co-operative national effort in which government in each of its three spheres and the panoply of resources and skills of civil society are marshalled, inspired and led. This can be achieved only if there is proper communication, especially by government. In order for it to be implemented optimally, a public health programme must be made known effectively to all concerned, down to the district nurse and patients. Indeed, for a public programme such as this to meet the constitutional requirement of reasonableness, its contents must be made known appropriately...

It is essential that there be a concerted national effort to combat the HIV/AIDS pandemic. The government has committed itself to such an effort. We have held that its policy fails to meet constitutional standards because it excludes those who could reasonably be included where such treatment is medically indicated to combat mother-to-child transmission of HIV.

That does not mean that everyone can immediately claim access to such treatment, although the ideal, as Dr Ntsabula says, is to achieve that goal. Every effort must, however, be made to do so as soon as reasonably possible. The increase in the budget to which we have referred will facilitate this... We consider it important that all sectors of the community in particular civil society, should co-operate in the steps taken to achieve this goal... The government has always respected and executed orders of this Court. There is no reason to believe that it will not do so in the present case.

8

Human Dignity and Proportionality

If my instants of discovery tend to occur in the bath-tub, my moments of being enlightened by others seem to happen in restaurants. At an evening meal in Johannesburg my dining companion was a Danish judge then on the European Court of Human Rights, Issy Foigel. He told me of a clear division of approach on his Court between judges from Southern Europe and those from Northern Europe. They might agree on outcomes, but their conceptual philosophies were quite different: judges from Southern Europe believed that their task was to distinguish between justice and injustice, between right and wrong, while judges from Northern Europe saw their function as being to hold the ring between competing claims of right. The latter felt that in a modern pluralistic democracy outright injustice was rare. In their view the basic problem of a human rights court was to find a principled way of balancing out the various public and private interests that came into conflict with each other, not to determine the frontiers between justice and injustice.

I came to see most of the work on my Court as involving claims between right and right. We were concerned not so much with classificatory frontiers between the lawful and the unlawful, as with reconciling the diverse interests that inevitably exist in an open and democratic society. In this setting abstract legal reasoning of a dogmatic kind gave way to a form of adjudication in which purpose, context, impact and values took centre-stage. This did not mean that principled legal argument and the maintenance of legal coherence gave way to vague and subjective notions of the good and the desirable. On the contrary, it became more necessary than ever to spell out the objective principles and factual material on which the judgment relied. And it was important to bear in mind that these principles themselves embodied and encoded the elements of balancing to which I have referred. Indeed, if I were to be stranded on a desert island and allowed to take only two constitutional elements with me, I would take human dignity and proportionality.

The difference between an approach derived from formal reasoning and one based on balancing was vividly brought home to me when Justice Antonin Scalia of the US Supreme Court and I were invited to speak at the sesquicentennial of the Danish Parliament. Clearly we were chosen with a view to providing a proportionate balance to each other. Arguing with characteristic force and clarity, Justice Scalia contended that the judge's role was limited to ensuring that the formal rules established by the Constitution were maintained. Individual liberty, he stated, was better protected by insisting on respect for the division of power between the States and the Federal Government on the one hand, and the separation of powers between legislature, executive, and the judiciary on the other, than by allowing judges to impose their subjective preferences on the democratically-arrived at decisions of the legislature. He was accordingly totally opposed to allowing concepts such as proportionality and balancing to become part of the judicial arsenal. In his view, it was for the legislators and not the judges to do the necessary balancing of interests and to arrive at the appropriate compromises. The occasion was most enjoyable, and I discovered three things: that sesquicentennial did not mean the 600th anniversary but the 150th; that Justice Scalia was as amiable off the Bench as he could be severe when on it; and that in the Danish setting the balancing approach to which Issy Foigel had introduced me seemed to strike a stronger chord than the one advanced by Justice Scalia. Though Denmark did not have a strong constitution, its place in the community of European nations, and its adherence to the European Convention on Human Rights, gave its people a strong sense of fundamental rights. And it was in France, where historically the general will of the people as expressed through Parliament had had strong sway, that I had heard a judge of the constitutional council make the following statement: the nineteenth century was a century where the executive took hold of the state; the twentieth century saw Parliament exert control over the executive; and the twenty-first century would be the century that saw the judiciary ensure that both parliament and the executive respected certain fundamental norms relating to the rights of the people.

The negotiated revolution which saw South Africa move from being an authoritarian, racist state to becoming a constitutional democracy led Professor Etienne Mureinik to make a memorable statement as far as the character of legal adjudication was concerned. He pointed out that we were crossing a bridge from a culture of authority to a culture of justification. Whether or not Justice Scalia's thinking can be said to belong to the culture of authority, our Court firmly located itself in the culture of justification. The implications for the judicial function turned out to be enormous. And it was our Court that was made responsible for guiding the legal community to embrace and internalize the necessary changes. Much more was involved than simply making a technical shift from what the lawyers call a literalist to a purposive approach to interpretation. The Constitution brought about a sea-change in the very nature of the judicial function. It required our Court to deal with three broad matters in a completely new way, one that could never have been envisaged in the pre-constitutional era. All three necessitated moving beyond an approach based on the application of purportedly inexorable rules towards accepting the duty in most matters for the judges to exercise constitutionally-controlled discretion. The transformation involved a journey from preoccupation with classification and strict adherence to formal rules to focussing on principled modes of weighing up the competing interests as triggered by the facts of the case and assessed in the light of the values of an open and democratic society. And to the extent that our Constitution encouraged us to look to foreign law, we discovered that the burgeoning of constitutional adjudication throughout the world tended to produce a similar evolution of judicial function.

In pre-constitutional times in our country Parliament had been sovereign, and the validity of its laws could never have been challenged. The main, if not exclusive, interpretive task of the courts had been to determine the intention of the legislature from the language it used when drafting the statute. Now the question of consistency with the Constitution became central. We were called upon to keep the legislation alive, even if some degree of strain had to be put on the language. The principal exercise, then, was not to determine from the words used what Parliament had meant, but rather to decide whether a reading of the text of the statute was possible which would ensure that the limits of constitutionality were not exceeded. The old and highly technical canons of construing statutes that had previously guided the legal community, became virtually redundant, and the very nature of legal debate and adjudication changed.

The second completely new area of judicial activity arose when, try as we might, the challenged statute could not reasonably be construed in a way that avoided placing a limitation on a right protected in the Constitution. We were now called upon to answer a question that had simply not been on the judicial agenda in pre-constitutional times: Was the limitation of the protected right justifiable in an open and democratic society based on human dignity, equality and freedom? In fact the issue of the justifiability of a legislative limitation of a right quickly came to occupy the bulk of our Court time. The Constitution itself provided a list of factors which could be relevant to this enquiry. In essence, we were required to exercise a judgment on a case-by-case basis using the principle of proportionality as our guide: Was the restriction on the right and the means used proportionate to the public interest to be served? At the heart of the exercise was the balancing of different interests, in a word, proportionality. Proportionality, proportionality, proportionality. I cannot repeat these words often enough—our very first case, dealing with the constitutionality of the death penalty, treated the principle of proportionality as the vertebral support of the whole legal analysis.

I will consider the significance of proportionality in some detail, but before doing so, I need to refer to the third seismic shift in the judicial function. It referred to the question of remedies. If the statute could not be read in a manner that was constitutionally compliant, and if the limitation of the right concerned could not be justified, what would the appropriate remedy be? The Constitution gave the Court a wide discretion in this regard, which it had to exercise judicially on a case-by-case basis. It could sever words from a statute that produced unconstitutionality, provided that what remained made sense and was consistent with the constitutional purpose of the statute. If words could not be blue-pencilled out in this way, the Court could declare notional unconstitutionality, that is, that the statute was unconstitutional to the extent that it purported to do X, Y, and Z. This was language quite unheard of in pre-constitutional days. And for those who remained embedded in the old legal practice of seeking maximum obedience to what the law-maker had had in mind, things got worse. We read words into a statute that had not been there before!

The first time we did this was in a case of an immigration statute that served a manifestly good public purpose, but was unconstitutional to the extent that it applied only to legally married people and did not include same-sex couples. After holding it to be unfairly discriminatory on the ground of sexual orientation, we decided not to send it back to Parliament for correction, but to save the law ourselves by adding a phrase to include same-sex life partnerships. The objectives of the law were clear, minimal textual interference was required and no significant budgetary consequences would follow. Parliament would inevitably have had to make the law compliant by adding the words that we read in. So, by keeping the law constitutionally alive, we were furthering rather than frustrating Parliament's objectives.

At a more general level, when declaring a statute to be invalid for failure to meet constitutional requirements, the Court was expressly empowered to add to this declaration any consequential order it deemed just and equitable. This gave the Court a wide discretion with regard to the appropriate remedy. The Constitution allowed it to keep an unconstitutional law alive for a certain period to give Parliament time to correct the defect, something unheard of before. This wide discretion did not release us from the obligation to provide sound reasons for our decisions. On the contrary, in each case we had to explain precisely what the competing considerations had been and set out fully the basis on which we had opted for a particular remedy or combination of remedies. Indeed, at our case conferences we would frequently spend as much if not more time on the question of remedies than on the substantive legal issues involved.

I return to the core substantive activity of the Court, which largely revolved around the application of the proportionality principle in the specific context of the case. In the end we had to make value judgments and we soon became aware of the need to spell out as fully and accurately as we could the basis for these judgments. They could not flow from the mere say-so or subjective visions of the judges. We had to establish the context which triggered the engagement with constitutional rights; analyse the public objectives sought to be served by the law in question; examine the extent to which its provisions protected rights; and, above all, determine whether the extent of the limitation was proportionate. In doing this balancing exercise we had to give considerable weight to the discretion that should properly be granted to government in its choice of the means to be used to achieve a legitimate purpose. We would also grant a certain margin of appreciation to government's capacity to make factual evaluations concerning social priorities and areas requiring legislative intervention. This discretion would be particularly relevant in sectors where the impact of a measure could be polycentric, that is, have a wide and not easily calculable effect on many spheres of life.

At the same time, we had always to gauge the measure concerned with the constitutional measuring-rod of what would be permissible in an open and democratic society based on human dignity, equality, and freedom. In applying this criterion we ranged far and wide, deriving as much benefit as we could from legal reasoning and legal practice in other parts of the world. We accordingly saw it as our duty to set out the judgments in such a way that the reader would know exactly what factors we had taken into account, what considerations had tipped the balance, and why.

In most cases we debated the issues until there was enough common ground for a unanimous judgment to be produced. But there were many times when we could not see eye-to-eye on the weight to be given to the different elements to be placed in the scales. Thus, our Court divided 6 to 5 when hearing a claim by Rastafari that their right to freedom of religion entitled them to exemption from a criminal prohibition against the use of marijuana. Though we all applied a balancing test we ended up giving different weights to the relevant factors. The case had been brought by a candidate attorney who was regarded by his professional order as fit and proper to join the profession, save for one fact: he had twice been convicted for possession of marijuana, and pursuant to his religion would not give an undertaking to desist from smoking it. The Court postponed the matter to receive extensive affidavits from law enforcement officials on the one hand, and the Rastafari on the other. After studying these materials, the majority of the court felt that there was no manageable way in which effectively to police the granting of an exemption to the Rastafari for purely religious purposes. Writing one of the dissenting judgments, I felt that the majority gave insufficient weight to what were in fact the existential claims of a marginalized religious group, thereby allowing mainstream thinking to get in the way of sustaining the principle of the right to be different. In my view, the police could manage the distribution of confiscated marijuana to designated Rastafari priests to use on sacramental occasions only. See the *Prince* case (p 216) for excerpts from judgments where the balancing was done in ways that produced different outcomes. What was important was that both the majority and the dissenting judgments fully set out the factors on which we respectively relied and the reasoning we followed.

Similarly, in equality cases we were required to take constitutionally-guided value judgments on whether differentiation between people on certain specified grounds amounted to unfair discrimination. To answer this question we found ourselves compelled to consider the substantive impact of the measures on members of the specified classes. Yet although we all applied the same proportionality test, we did not always arrive as the same conclusion. Thus, the Court divided 7 to 3 in a case that turned on whether a statute that restricted a right to maintenance from the estate of a deceased person, to surviving spouses only, discriminated unfairly against unmarried co-habitants. In essence, the majority held that because the law had attached no legal obligation to support an unmarried partner during the deceased's lifetime, it would be incongruous and unfair to make the estate liable after the death of the deceased.

A dissenting judgment which I wrote was, embarrassingly for me, more than twice as long as the majority judgment. It stated that the issue should not be assessed within the narrow confines of matrimonial law, but rather according to the broader principles of family law. The key ingredients should be the nature and intensity of the familial relationship, the intimacy of the partners, and the extent to which the need for maintenance flowed from a selfless devotion to the deceased and the children that had limited the survivor's possibilities of accumulating her or his own assets. A major difference between me and my colleagues turned upon the weight to be given to the fact that in legal terms, if not always in reality, people are free to choose whether to marry. See the *Volks* case (p 224) for excerpts explaining our different positions.

Then we had matters involving the enforcement of social and economic rights, where the key question was whether the state had taken reasonable measures within its available resources progressively to realize the right concerned, a matter discussed in Chapter Nine. Proportionality, fairness, reasonableness: these were not questions that could be decided purely by grammatical textual analysis and logical inference. In just about every case that came before us, the Constitution obliged us to make value judgments on issues of major social and moral importance. The problem then was not *whether* to make value judgments, but *how* to do so in a principled way that was true to the letter and spirit of the Constitution. Our Constitution is intensely value-laden. The values are not only implicit in its overall democratic design. They are explicitly set out in the Preamble, the founding provisions and the manner in which the Bill of Rights has to be interpreted.

See Appendix 1 (Preamble, s 1(1) and s 39(1) and (2)). See also the *Rustenburg* case (p 229).

It will be seen from the two cases cited above, dealing respectively with the rights of a marginalized religious group and unmarried co-habitants, that the members of the Court would not necessarily have disagreed in their personal capacities as to what policies would be best for all concerned. The same would have applied in relation to prostitution/sex work. What divided the court was whether or not the matters lay purely within the discretion of the legislature, or whether fundamental rights were involved calling for the courts to intervene. Normally it is not for judges, but for the elected legislature, to decide on public policy and how resources should best be used. This is not simply because of the need not to get involved in questions affecting the budget. The enforcement of basic civil rights will, after all, often involve intrusion on the budget, such as when the court orders the holding of elections or the provision of legal aid. The deeper question is whether it is institutionally appropriate for judges to take positions on highly controversial questions of the kind that are hotly debated during elections. The answer must in general be no. Whether government policy is wise or stupid is something for public opinion and the electorate to decide, not for the judges. In a constitutional democracy this must be the general rule. I stress, the general rule, not the invariable one.

My view is that there are indeed a restricted number of circumstances involving highly contentious matters where it is actually an advantage for judges not to be accountable to the electorate. We have a constitutional duty to defend deep core values which are part of emerging world jurisprudence, and which relate directly to evolving constitutional notions in our own country. This makes me sharply aware of the manner in which the Constitution connects the maintenance of judicial independence and the protection of human dignity. The very notion of entrenching rights is to provide a basic framework of constitutional regard for every human being. It is not the duty of courts to side with one section of society against another, however powerful or weak. Nor may they permit purely personal opinions on political, social and moral questions to hold sway. Of course judges have opinions, frequently very strong ones, but any influence these opinions may have, needs to be refracted through the prism of constitutional reasoning. And it is the Constitution itself that makes it incumbent on judges to continue to see to it that basic respect for the dignity of every person is maintained at all times. That is why we have fundamental rights.

Respect for human dignity is the unifying constitutional principle for a society that is not only particularly diverse, but extremely unequal. This implies that the Bill of Rights exists not simply to ensure that the 'haves' can continue to have, but to help create conditions in which the basic dignity of the 'have nots' can be secured. The key question, then, is not whether unelected judges should ever take positions on controversial political questions. It is to define in a principled way the limited and functionally manageable circumstances in which the judicial responsibility for being the ultimate protector of human dignity compels judges to enter what might be politically-contested terrain. It is precisely in situations where political leaders may have difficulty withstanding constitutionally undue populist pressure, and where human dignity is most at risk, that it becomes an advantage that judges are not accountable to the electorate.

It is at these moments that the judicial function expresses itself in its purest form. Judges, able to rely on the independence guaranteed to them by the Constitution, ensure that justice as constitutionally envisaged is done to all, without fear, favour or prejudice.

In securing protection of the rights of particularly vulnerable groups, courts will be guided by values rooted in the text and spirit of the Constitution. It is not by chance that most work done by most courts with constitutional jurisdiction in the world is concerned with conducting balancing exercises conducted in the context of constitutionally-dictated values. One size does not fit all. Proportionality has its own exigencies, its own logic, its own evidential requirements, its own cluster of guiding factors. Decisions on proportionality are strongly influenced by generalized notions of what would be permissible in an open and democratic society. Such a society is a notional one. It is not to be found in this country or that. It does not have this particular constitution or that, this kind of judiciary or that. It is an ideal type of society, constructed out of the actual experience of the way issues of power and of rights are dealt with in countries that are widely regarded as democratic. This society repudiates forms of oppression, hardship, division and discrimination that have been known in the past (and, sadly, are still current in many parts of the world today). It acknowledges the foundational character of the principle of human dignity, and aspires to accept people for who they are. It presupposes diversity and welcomes and treats everyone with equal concern and respect. It is a society that protects rights of conscience and speech. It is one that ensures that government is accountable to the people, that every vote counts equally, and that minority voices can be heard.

This imagined society then becomes the template for measuring the constitutionality of governmental laws and conduct. Reference to the qualities of such a society frequently tips the scales in the borderline cases that typically reach us. Our whole life as lawyers and human beings prepares us for discerning and appreciating the lineaments of this society. As Oliver Wendell Holmes said of the common law a century ago, the lifeblood of constitutional law comes not from logic but from experience. The same can now be said of constitutional law, with the additional observation that its sinews come from logic and that its overall coherence and sustainability come from the manner in which logic and experience are fused.

The *Prince* Case

It will be seen from the excerpts below that the majority and I agreed on the need to do a balancing exercise. On the one side of the scales were the claims of the Rastafari for an exemption to enable them to engage in their religious practice of smoking marijuana (dagga). On the other was the feasibility or otherwise of law enforcement agencies being able effectively to police a limited exemption in their favour. The majority were of the view that granting a limited exemption would make effective law enforcement impossible and that in any event a limited exemption would not satisfy the claims of the Rastafari. My judgment held that the majority did not give enough weight to the concept of religious freedom for a marginalized group, and to the importance to society as a whole of tolerating difference. Furthermore, in the balancing exercise it was necessary to distinguish a severely noxious drug like heroin from a drug on a par with liquor and tobacco, that had been produced from an indigenous plant that had been used for recreational purposes since pre-colonial times.

THE MAJORITY:

The question is not whether we agree with the law prohibiting the possession and use of cannabis. Our views in that regard are irrelevant. The only question is whether the law is inconsistent with the Constitution. The appellant contends that it is because it interferes with his right to freedom of religion and his right to practise his religion. It is to that question that we now turn.

In the proportionality analysis required by the Constitution, there can be no doubt that the right to freedom of religion and to practise religion are important rights in an open and democratic society based on human dignity, equality and freedom, and that the disputed legislation places a substantial limitation on the religious practices of Rastafari. It must also be accepted that the legislation serves an important governmental purpose in the war against drugs. In substance, the appellant contends that the legislation, though legitimate in its purpose and application to the general public, is overbroad because it has been formulated in a way that brings within its purview the use of cannabis by Rastafari that is legitimate and ought not to be prohibited.

The unchallenged general prohibition in the disputed legislation against the possession or use of harmful drugs is directed in the first instance to cutting off the supply of such drugs to potential users. It seeks to address the harm caused by the drug problem by denying all possession of prohibited substances (other than for medical and research purposes) and not by seeking to penalise only the harmful use of such substances. This facilitates the enforcement of the legislation. Persons found in possession of the drug are guilty of an offence, whether they intend to use it for themselves or not, and irrespective of whether its eventual use will indeed be harmful. This method of control is actually prescribed by the 1961 Single Convention on Narcotic Drugs to which South Africa is a party.

Cannabis is a drug in which there is a substantial illicit trade which exists within South Africa and internationally. Moreover, the use to which cannabis is put by Rastafari is not simply the sacramental or symbolic consumption of a small quantity at a religious ceremony. It is used communally and privately, during religious ceremonies when two or more Rastafari come together, and at other times and places. According to his own evidence, the appellant uses cannabis regularly at his home and elsewhere. All that distinguishes his use of cannabis from the general use that is prohibited, is the purpose for which he uses the drug, and the self-discipline that he asserts in not abusing it.

There is no objective way in which a law enforcement official could distinguish between the use of cannabis for religious purposes and the use of cannabis for recreation. It would be even more difficult, if not impossible, to distinguish objectively between the possession of cannabis for the one or the other of the above purposes. Nor is there any objective way in which a law enforcement official could determine whether a person found in possession of cannabis, who says that it is possessed for religious purposes, is genuine or not. Indeed, in the absence of a carefully controlled chain of permitted supply, it is difficult to imagine how the island of legitimate acquisition and use by Rastafari for the purpose of practicing their religion could be distinguished from the surrounding ocean of illicit trafficking and use.

[T]he religious use of cannabis cannot be equated to medical use. It would expose Rastafari to the same harm as others are exposed to by using cannabis, depending only on their self discipline to use it in ways that avoid such harm. Moreover, to make its use for religious purposes dependent upon a permit issued by the state to 'bona fide Rastafari' would, in the circumstances of the present case, be inconsistent with the freedom of religion. It is the essence of that freedom that individuals have a choice that does not depend in any way upon the permission of the executive . . . [A] permit system would not address the law enforcement problems...Ensuring that the use of cannabis fell within the conditions of the permit would depend entirely upon the self-discipline of the holder and would not be amenable to state monitoring or control. There is, of course, the pervading anomaly that permission for Rastafari to possess cannabis is meaningless unless they are allowed to grow it...

The use made of cannabis by Rastafari cannot in the circumstances be sanctioned without impairing the state's ability to enforce its legislation in the interests of the public at large and to honour its international obligation to do so. The failure to make provision for an exemption in respect of the possession and use of cannabis by Rastafari is thus reasonable and justifiable under our Constitution.

The granting of a limited exemption interferes materially with the ability of the state to enforce its legislation, yet, if the use of cannabis were limited to the purpose of the exemption, it would fail to meet the needs of the Rastafari religion.

SACHS J:

Intolerance may come in many forms. At its most spectacular and destructive it involves the use of power to crush beliefs and practices considered alien and threatening. At its more benign it may operate through a set of rigid mainstream norms which do not permit the possibility of alternative forms of conduct.

By concluding that the granting even of a limited exemption in favour of the Rastafari would interfere materially with the ability of the state to enforce anti-drug legislation, the majority judgment effectively, and in my view unnecessarily, subjects the Rastafari community to a choice between their faith and respect for the law. Exemptions from general laws always impose some cost on the state, yet practical inconvenience and disturbance of established majoritarian mind-sets are the price that constitutionalism exacts from government. In my view the majority judgment puts a thumb on the scales in favour of ease of law enforcement, and gives insufficient weight to the impact the measure will have, not only on the fundamental rights of the appellant and his religious community, but on the basic notion of tolerance and respect for diversity that our Constitution demands for and from all in our society.

[T]he weighing of the respective interests at stake does not take place on weightless scales of pure logic pivoted on a friction-free fulcrum of abstract rationality. The balancing has to be done in the context of a lived and experienced historical, sociological and imaginative reality. Even if for purposes of making its judgment the Court is obliged to classify issues in conceptual terms and abstract itself from such reality, it functions with materials drawn from that reality and has to take account of the impact of its judgments on persons living within that reality. Moreover, the Court itself is part of that reality and must engage in a complex process of simultaneously detaching itself from and engaging with it. I believe that in the present matter, history, imagination and mind-set play a particularly significant role, especially with regard to the weight to be given to the various factors in the scales.

For the purposes of balancing, some laws (or parts of laws) will of necessity be more equal than others. Thus, the problems the state might have in enforcing a general ban on heroin might be no different to those it has in interdicting dagga use. Yet in the balancing exercise the impact of the former on law enforcement will weigh by far the more heavily. A retreat on the tiny front of sacramental use by Rastafari of indigenous and long-used dagga might make little if any difference to prosecution of the major battles against cartels importing heroin, cocaine and mandrax. Indeed the 'war on drugs' might be better served if instead of seeking out and apprehending Rastafari whose other-worldly use of dagga renders them particularly harmless rather than harmful or harmed, such resources were dedicated to the prohibition of manifestly harmful drugs.

What is required is the maximum harmonisation of all the competing considerations, on a principled yet nuanced and flexible case-by-case basis, located in South African reality yet guided by international experience, articulated with appropriate candour and accomplished without losing sight of the ultim-ate values highlighted by our Constitution. In achieving this balance, this Court may frequently find itself faced with com-plex problems as to what properly belongs to the discretionary sphere which the Constitution allocates to the legislature and the executive, and what falls squarely to be determined by the judiciary.

The Rastafari are not an established religious group whose interests no legislature would dare ignore. One may compare their position to that of major faiths. Thus, in the period when the racist liquor laws forbade Africans generally to possess liquor, the power of the Christian Church was such that access to communion wine was granted to African congregants (just as in the USA even at the height of prohibition the use of com-munion wine was exempted). On the other hand, Africans who sought to brew beer as part of traditional religious supplica-tion rites were prosecuted. The difference of treatment lay not in the nature of the activity or exemption, but in the status of the religious groups involved. One must conclude that in the area of claims freely to exercise religion, it is not familiarity, but unfamiliarity, that breeds contempt.

One cannot imagine in South Africa today any legislative authority passing or sustaining laws which suppressed central beliefs and practices of Christianity, Islam, Hinduism and Judaism. These are well-organized religions, capable of mounting strong lobbies and in a position materially to affect the outcome of elections. They are not driven to seek constitutional protection from the courts.

[N]o amount of formal constitutional analysis can in itself resolve the problem of balancing matters of faith against matters of public interest. Yet faith and public interest overlap and intertwine in the need to protect tolerance as a constitutional virtue and respect for diversity and openness as a constitutional principle. Religious tolerance is accordingly not only important to those individuals who are saved from having to make excruciating choices between their beliefs and the law. It is deeply meaningful to all of us because religion and belief matter, and because living in an open society matters.

The central issue in this case has accordingly not been whether or not we approve or disapprove of the use of dagga, or whether we are believers or non-believers, or followers of this particular denomination or that. Indeed, in the present case the clarion call of tolerance could resonate with particular force for those of us who may in fact be quite puritan about the use of dagga and who, though respectful of all faiths, might not be adherents of any religion at all, let alone sympathetic to the tenets of Rastafari belief and practice. The call echoes for all who see reasonable accommodation of difference not simply as a matter of astute jurisprudential technique which facilitates settlement of disputes, but as a question of principle central to the whole constitutional enterprise.

The test of tolerance as envisaged by the Bill of Rights comes not in accepting what is familiar and easily accommodated, but in giving reasonable space to what is 'unusual, bizarre or even threatening'.

The *Volks* Case

The question was whether unmarried co-habitants were unfairly discriminated against on the ground of marital status because they were excluded from the benefits of the Surviving Spouses Maintenance Act. The majority of the Court said there was no unfairness. The two women judges who sat in the matter dissented. I also dissented. The excerpts below show the difference between the majority judgment written by Justice Thembile Skweyiya, and my judgment.

SKWEYIYA J:

Marriage and family are important social institutions in our society. Marriage has a central and special place, and forms one of the important bases for family life in our society.

The distinction between married and unmarried people cannot be said to be unfair when considered in the larger context of the rights and obligations uniquely attached to marriage. Whilst there is a reciprocal duty of support between married persons, no duty of support arises by operation of law in the case of unmarried cohabitants. The maintenance benefit in . . . the Act falls within the scope of the maintenance support obligation attached to marriage. The Act applies to persons in respect of whom the deceased person (spouse) would have remained legally liable for maintenance, by operation of law, had he or she not died.

Marriage is not merely a piece of paper. Couples who choose to marry enter the agreement fully cognisant of the legal obligations which arise by operation of law upon the conclusion of the marriage. These obligations arise as soon as the marriage is concluded, without the need for any further agreement. They include obligations that extend beyond the termination of marriage and even after death. To the extent that any obligations arise between cohabitants during the subsistence of their relationship, these arise by agreement and only to the extent of that agreement. The Constitution does not require the imposition of an obligation on the estate of a deceased person, in circumstances where the law attaches no such obligation during the deceased's lifetime, and there is no intention on the part of the deceased to undertake such an obligation.

I conclude that it is not unfair to make a distinction between survivors of a marriage on the one hand, and survivors of a heterosexual cohabitation relationship on the other. In the context of the provision for maintenance of the survivor of a marriage by the estate of the deceased, it is entirely appropriate not to impose a duty upon the estate where none arose by operation of law during the lifetime of the deceased. Such an imposition would be incongruous, unfair, irrational and untenable.

I have a genuine concern for vulnerable women who cannot marry despite the fact that they wish to and who become the victims of cohabitation relationships. I do not think however that their cause is truly assisted by an extension of the Act or that vulnerable women would be unfairly discriminated against if this were not done. The answer lies in legal provisions that will make a real difference to vulnerable women at a time when both partners to the relationship are still alive. Once provision is made for this, the legal context in which section 2(1) falls to be evaluated will change drastically.

SACHS J:

[S]hould a person who has shared her home and life with her deceased partner, borne and raised children with him, cared for him in health and in sickness, and dedicated her life to support the family they created together, be treated as a legal stranger to his estate, with no claim for subsistence because they were never married? Should marriage be the exclusive touchstone of a survivor's legal entitlement as against the rights of legatees and heirs?

The question of the fairness of excluding non-married survivors from benefits falls to be assessed not in the narrow confines of the rules established by matrimonial law, but rather within the broader and more situation-sensitive framework of the principles of family law, principles that are evolving rapidly in our new constitutional era.

[T]he general purpose of family law is to promote stability, responsibility and equity in intimate family relations.

The purpose of the Act was to provide a statutory claim against the estate for recently bereaved widows in need. The key ingredients are the familial relationship, intimacy and need. Taking them in combination, to exclude the survivor simply because she has no marriage certificate, is not only socially harsh, it is legally unfair.

... [W]hile it is true that caring for one's family is one of life's great joys, and as such calls for no extra reward, fairness does not inevitably translate into sacrifice.

The purpose of constitutional law is to convert misfortune to be endured into injustice to be remedied. It would indeed be a perverse interpretation of family law that obliged one to disregard the fact that the circumstances of need in which a typical survivor might find herself, were produced precisely by her selfless devotion to the deceased and their family during his lifetime. [I]t is socially unrealistic, unduly moralistic and hence constitutionally unfair, for the Act to discriminate against the powerless and economically dependent party, now threatened with destitution, on the basis that she should either have insisted on marriage or else withdrawn from the relationship.

The issues are not simple. There is a great social need to promote marriage as an institution which provides stability, security and predictability for intimate family relations. All measures aimed at redistribution of such uneven loads, whether through family law or welfare law, risk being criticised as being calculated to undermine self-reliance. Yet, while over-paternalism can be disempowering and negate the very objective of achieving equality, what has disparagingly been called the concept of judicial tough love can be unduly insensitive to the actual and overwhelming problems people have had to face in life. The knowledge that the law will intervene to provide basic justice will in fact assist such people to overcome a sense of helplessness and fatalism. That, indeed, is why courts intervene to protect fundamental rights. In so doing they enhance rather than undermine dignity and self-respect.

The reality against which the Act must be interpreted is that many recently bereaved, elderly, and poor women find themselves with no assets or savings other than their clothing and cooking utensils, little chance of employment and only the prospect of a state old-age pension to keep them from penury.

Their choice has been between destitution, prostitution and loneliness, on the one hand, and continuing cohabitation with a person who was unwilling or unable to marry them on the other. Any consideration of the fairness or otherwise of excluding from maintenance claims people who chose the latter path, must take account of this.

It follows that the continued blanket exclusion of domestic partners from the ambit of the Act, irrespective of the degree of commitment shown to the family by the survivor, cannot be justified. The Act is accordingly invalid to the extent that it excludes unmarried survivors of permanent intimate life partnerships as identified above, from pursuing claims for maintenance.

The *Rustenburg Platinum Mines* Case

This case turned on the principles to be used when reviewing decisions by an arbitrator appointed in terms of labour legislation to determine the fairness of a dismissal from employment. At the hearing much of the debate turned on whether to apply the relatively narrow grounds of review permitted by labour legislation or the wider grounds of review allowed for by administrative law. My judgment contended that in fact the processes were of a hybrid nature, and that whether the case was approached through the door of labour law or the portal of administrative law the outcome should be the same. What should be decisive were the values of an open and democratic society. Values and text could not be separated.

SACHS J:

The values of the Constitution are strong, explicit and clearly intended to be considered part of the very texture of the constitutional project. They are implicit in the very structure and design of the new democratic order. The letter and the spirit of the Constitution cannot be separated: just as the values are not free-floating, ready to alight as mere adornments on this or that provision, so is the text not self-supporting, awaiting occasional evocative enhancement. The role of constitutional values is certainly not simply to provide a patina of virtue to otherwise bald, neutral and discrete legal propositions. Text and values work together in integral fashion to provide the protection promised by the Constitution.

In a value-based constitutional democracy with a normative structure that is seamless, organic and ever-evolving, the manner in which claims to constitutional justice are typified and dealt with should always be integrated within the context of the setting, interests and values involved.

9

The Secular and the Sacred: The Dual Challenges of Same-sex Marriage

Introduction: the March

It was November 1991, some years before I became a judge, and I was sweating. After 24 years of exile, I was once more driving towards the centre of Cape Town, and perspiration poured down my back. November in Cape Town is hot, and I was at the wheel for almost the first time after having been nearly killed in Mozambique by the bomb put in my car by South African security agents. So I was nervous and scared about driving with one hand only. And I was sweating because I didn't know the roads very well—there were new one-way streets—and we had been told to meet at 'the usual meeting place', but I, the big freedom fighter, didn't even know where the usual meeting place was. But above all I was sweating because I was going to be taking part in my first Gay Pride march.

I was late, and I could imagine the organizers saying 'Oh well, Albie's going to duck out again'. They had held a march in Johannesburg the year before, and invited me along because of my widely publicized position against discrimination on grounds of sexual orientation—but when it had come to actually marching in support of the principle I had said sorry, but there was a heterosexual marriage I had to attend on that day. Fortunately the bridal couple were well known, so the organizers had understood that this hadn't been an excuse...But not to turn up a second time...?

Suddenly in the heart of town I saw the marchers coming towards me. I didn't know where to park, so I slipped into St George's Cathedral parking area, thinking that the Archbishop could forgive me for parking illegally there just this once. I look at the marchers. The first poster says 'Suck—Don't Swallow'. My first thought was, Oh No, I'll be in the newspaper tomorrow! Can't I be carrying a placard that says 'Straights for Gays'— why don't they have a section for people like us? And then I am ashamed of my embarrassment. I am still not too strong after the bomb, and lope clumsily along to catch up with the marchers. I see Professor Edwin Cameron, whom I knew from legal conferences, and fall in at his side. And a wonderful feeling overcomes me...I have crossed a barrier, and feel proud, at home, and comfortable being on this march.

We carried on for maybe another 20 minutes, ending up in a small grassy area called de Waal Park, where I had played as a child. An impromptu meeting was held—it was not a huge mass rally, maybe 200 people—and I was a little anxious, because I had another meeting later that day, and they called upon me to be an early speaker. The first thought that came to me was that I had played in that park as a child, and later on I had seen signs that said 'Whites Only'. These were the visible signs. But there were also invisible signs that could have read 'Straights Only'. Straight couples could hold hands, could cuddle, could express their intimacy quite comfortably in that park, but same-sex couples knew that if they did so, the police would be onto them. I shared that memory with the audience, and said that the theme of equality for gays and lesbians was important for members of a community that had long been denied their full humanity in our society. But its significance was much greater than that. It was important for our whole country, because we are a country of diverse people. Difference was part and parcel of the very character of South Africa, and how our nation handled difference was going to be key to how our nation survived and prospered. And so this march had raised questions that went beyond getting rid of a form of hurtful apartheid directed at a certain section of the population. It went to the heart of the open society which the new democratic constitution should try to promote. And then I rushed off to my other meeting.

Christian Lawyers for Africa

In 2005—and the relevance of this prelude will become clear—we were having a meeting of the Justices of the Constitutional Court, and Chief Justice Pius Langa said that he had received a request from a body called Christian Lawyers for Africa, inviting him to attend the opening of their conference in Johannesburg. But it was to be held during the court recess and he would be in Fiji helping to solve the constitutional crisis there, so was there anybody else who could go? We looked around the table. No volunteers. Eventually I tentatively put up my hand and said 'Pius, I'll be here, I can go, but I don't think I'm the right person to attend that conference.' He shook his head. 'No,' he answered 'you are *exactly* the right person.' Pius, the son of a preacher, is a Christian, a lawyer, and an African, but I suspected he didn't want to attend the conference in that sectarian capacity. I understood and agreed to welcome the lawyers from all over the continent on behalf of the Chief Justice and the Court.

When some weeks later I was being driven to the conference, I wasn't sweating, because it wasn't a hot time of year. But I was tense and nervous, thinking about the welcoming address I was scheduled to make. The tension diminished at seeing a hall filled with men and women from all over the continent, resplendently dressed in the different costumes of Africa—comfortable expression of diversity always warms my heart. Yet I continued to be uneasy, because I didn't want to give just a polite formal welcome. These were people of conscience. They were entitled to a real message of welcome from a robust and active Court that defended our new Constitution, an expansive, meaningful Constitution that had been achieved with much difficulty. Surely I should say something that linked the spirit and the character of our work with the intensity of their beliefs. And as I looked around, I knew how I should begin.

I would tell them about the difficulty I had had when it came to being sworn in, in the presence of Nelson Mandela, as a judge of the Constitutional Court in 1994. So when called to the podium, I explained that after undertaking to uphold the Constitution without fear, favour or prejudice and to do justice to all, there were two ways of swearing the oath: you could affirm, which you did simply by saying 'I affirm', or you could raise your right arm and say 'So help me God'. Choosing between them raised a profound dilemma of conscience for me. I had grown up in a very, very secular home. My parents had fought with their parents on questions of religion. They had taken what they had regarded as a deeply principled stand against what they had seen as an improved ideology, a set of rules and principles, that they just hadn't been able to go along with. The consequences had proved very difficult for me as a child, in a school which was half-Christian, half-Jewish, being the one child who was a Jew (I am a Jew) but who was not religious, not practising in any way. I had felt that to pretend a belief simply to be accepted by the other boys would have been disrespectful to myself, to my own conscience and above all disrespectful to God, if God existed.

The result was that at an early age my conscience was fashioned by the question of belief, and by the centrality of belief in establishing who you were as a person. The issue of racial injustice in South Africa was, in fact, far less complicated for my evolving consciousness—my mother worked as a typist for an African leader Moses Kotane, and it was obvious to me from my earliest years that inequality was detestable. But exploring deep interior thoughts about God, and refusing to pretend a belief I didn't have, that was hard. One result was to implant in me a life-long respect for believers of every kind. Though when pressed I would call myself a non-believer, I did in fact have a strong set of beliefs, my own world view, in many ways a deeply spiritual one with overwhelming ethical implications. These beliefs were to affect everything about my life, whom I married, where I lived, ultimately even my physical shape. But they were not structured around invocation of a faith, and did not express themselves within the confines of any organized religion.

I told the audience that as a consequence of my preoccupation with questions of conscience, when it came to constitutional negotiations in the 1990s, I was the one to be able to offer a solution to what many people had thought would be a totally intractable problem: the wording of the Preamble to the Constitution. Many negotiators insisted that the Constitution should begin with the words: 'In humble submission to Almighty God.' And for the seventy per cent of South Africans who regarded themselves as Christian, frequently very devout, for the five per cent or more of Muslim or Hindu persuasion, for the many Jews and people of other faiths, not to have invoked recognition of the deity in the most solemn of all public documents, would have been to devalue it. Without these words the Constitution would for them have been just another document devoid of special and deep connection with the inner convictions of the great majority of the nation. On the other hand, for the people who had grown up without being religious, or for whom faith had receded into the background, the idea of opening the most worldly of all documents, the most people-centred, the most human-created, with an invocation of that kind, would have been profoundly oppressive. And the solution had come to me quickly. I had said 'We (I was then on the Constitutional committee in the ANC) open our meetings with a hymn, Nkosi Sikelel' iAfrika—we sing it as the hymn of the oppressed people, the anthem of hope for our country. We sing it if we're black or white, believers or non-believers. It's become the song of the future. Let the Constitution contain the phrase 'Nkosi Sikelel' iAfrika, God Seën Suid-Afrika, God Bless Africa—in all the eleven official languages.' The idea was accepted, and far from the invocation serving to divide our population, it became an element that united us. And now you see our Rugby team singing the anthem, getting the words right, Nkosi Sikelel' iAfrika—white, black players—all singing together. Religious believers feel that there is recognition of the importance of their belief. Non-believers accept that this is a South African hymn, part of our history, part of the emerging texture of our nation.

I explained this to the delegates, and returned to the scene where the judges were solemnly being sworn in. Being alphabetically challenged, I would come last. Five of the official languages were used. And my dilemma was: What do I do when taking the oath? If I am to follow my conscience as developed in childhood, if I am to be faithful to the way I grew up, to my true beliefs, I will simply affirm. Yet on this most special of all occasions I feel a need to raise what remains left of my right arm. This is the arm that represents close friends who didn't survive to see freedom: Ruth First, Joe Gqabi, Looksmart Solwande, Elija Loza, all assassinated or tortured to death. It is the most solemn part of my body, and raising it would give deep meaning and significance to my adjuration—to use a legal word—to uphold the Constitution without fear or favour. And so, I told the delegates, I raised my right arm and I said 'So help me God'. The Christian Lawyers for Africa stood up and cheered. Speaker after speaker thereafter referred to what I had said. I was bemused. I had told the most ardent of believers that I was not a believer, and yet they had given me a standing ovation...

The next morning about seventy-five of them came to visit the Constitutional Court and I took them on a tour of our beautiful building. After nearly two hours the tour is over, and I say good-bye—I've enjoyed taking them around, people from my continent, lawyers like myself, but I have to rush off now to another meeting. (I always seem to be rushing off to meetings. I once thought that freedom meant no more meetings—did I get that one wrong!) And I'm late. The other gathering is in the nearby women's jail, which has now been converted into a site of memory where the Commission for Gender Equality has its offices. But the visitors throng around me: 'Please, you can't go, we must say a prayer for you.' And there are short prayers, and medium prayers, and long prayers—and the long prayer isn't just wishing me well, it's putting in a lot of what the person concerned believes about the world. And I'm moved by the long, long prayer, because it is honestly communicated within the framework of the values of those surrounding me. They are wishing me well, and doing so from their innermost selves. At last the prayer comes to an end, and I'm just about to rush off, when they say 'No—we must lay on hands.' Now, more than seventy-five people laying on hands takes time, and only after they have all laid on their hands, do I finally rush off to the women's jail.

I relate this story because, more than any other case in this Court, the same-sex marriages matter forced me to think actively about the strange connections between life and law. We have a text, we have a Constitution, we have a defined role to uphold the Constitution. Yet there are so many ways to apply the Constitution to a particular problem. How did the two experiences, on the surface so contradictory, representing two deep and apparently conflicting motor forces, play themselves out in the judgment I wrote, I wondered.

'Manipulators' versus 'Bigots'?

I had been asked by the Chief Justice to do the first draft for the Court. I don't think that at any time when preparing the draft I consciously referred to either of the above experiences.

But experience is experience—it becomes part of your being, it shapes your responses and your reactions, your intuitions, the way you tend to lean one way or the other when choosing between different forms of persuasive reasoning, each with its own internal rationality, that lead to different outcomes. At a deep level of my consciousness I was eager to find a way of accommodating the intense significance of the case for both communities: the gay and lesbian community seeking to be free, to be emancipated, to have shackles removed, to be able to enjoy their full humanity; and the large community of sincere believers for whom recognition of same-sex marriages was anathema—something distressing, disturbing, threatening. The judgment should attempt to speak with equal voice to both groups. It should not implicitly regard the one as a manipulative lobby group, or the other as a bunch of benighted bigots (counsel for the different parties had at times strayed towards implying these descriptions). Once you start dividing the community for whom the Constitution works into 'goodies' and 'baddies', then I think you wander away from the heart of the constitutional enterprise. To discover the humanity, the integrity, the honesty in everybody, and to present your response in a way that everybody can say 'I understand what is being said; I have grave doubts about the result; but the judgment acknowledges what I'm thinking, knows where I am, and takes account of my convictions and respects my conscience and dignity; I'm not being defined out of the answer by what purports to be a completely neutral way of framing issues and arriving at conclusions; my convictions, values and perspectives are being taken seriously and treated thoughtfully and with respect.'

I had written judgments in earlier cases dealing with claims by religious communities that they be exempt on grounds of religious belief from the general terms of governmental statutes. While doing research in the USA, the UK and South Africa, I had encountered a deep sense of indignation running through the writings of scholars, many of whom were simultaneously deeply religious and socially progressive. What wounded them was a notion they detected in mainstream legal literature that somehow the public realm was confined to a world of rationality, of public reason, that all forward-looking people could understand. Religion, on the other hand was segregated-off to a nook where people were free to pursue as a matter of private conscience whatever personal beliefs they might have. They objected to what they saw as the expulsion of religion from the public realm. And so the toughest part of the case for me was not purely technical; it was to take religion seriously as part of public life, and to respond to both the gay and lesbian community and the religious communities in a balanced, principled and carefully reasoned way. All had the right to feel that their claims and convictions had been subjected to thoughtful and sensitive constitutional inquiry.

Ms Fourie and Ms Bonthuys

Marie Fourie and Cecelia Bonthuys had presented a simple story to the Court. They had met, been attracted to each other, started going out, and then lived together for ten years. Regarded as a couple by all their friends, they decided to get married. The Marriage Officer told them that he personally had no problems about celebrating their marriage, but there was an insuperable difficulty: the vow that they would have to take followed the question: 'Do you, AB, take CD to be your lawful husband/ wife?' In his view the words husband and wife prevented him from solemnizing the marriage. The couple took the matter to the High Court. The judge was not unsympathetic. He accepted that the Constitution expressly included sexual orientation as one of the grounds of forbidden unfair discrimination, together with disability, race, colour, creed, national origin, birth, marital status. They were all are there. Yet he could not instruct the Marriage Officer to marry them as long as the statute stood in their way. So they then took the judge's decision to the Supreme Court of Appeal. One of the judgments in that Court gave them a tiny modicum of success. It was written by Edwin Cameron, next to whom I had marched in Cape Town. After acknowledging that the statute created obstacles to same-sex marriages, he pointed out that it nevertheless permitted church officials appointed as Marriage Officers to marry people according to the tenets of their religion; and indeed there were some churches created expressly for gay and lesbian congregations. Even if the clergy in the churches had not yet been recognized by the Minister for Home Affairs as Marriage Officers, it was foreseeable that in future they would be so empowered. The effect was to open a tiny window for the celebration at some future date of legally recognized same-sex marriages.

In the meanwhile the Gay and Lesbian Project had brought a case in the Johannesburg High Court challenging the constitutionality of the statute inasmuch as it effectively excluded same-sex couples from the right to marry. The High Court judge decided to postpone hearing the matter until the Constitutional

Court had ruled on the appeal in *Fourie,* and the papers in his case were sent on to us. We consolidated the two cases and heard them together.

The Court was packed. There were journalists from many international agencies, as well as supporters and opponents of same-sex marriages. At times counsel arguing before us became emotional, but generally the tone was restrained. Counsel for Ms Fourie and the Gay and Lesbian Project contended that the common law and the Marriage Act discriminated unfairly against same-sex couples, and that the Court should develop the common law and read in the gender-neutral word 'spouse' into the Act so as to permit same-sex couples to marry. Counsel for the state argued in reply that there might well be a lacuna (gap) in the law, but even if the common law and the statute did discriminate unfairly, it was a matter where public opinion needed to be consulted, and the remedy should be provided by Parliament, not the Court. *Amici curiae* (friends of the Court) who appeared on behalf of the Catholic Church and a body called Doctors for Life, argued intensely for protecting marriage as an institution aimed at procreation, which had been historically created with an intrinsically religious character.

It would not be appropriate for me to publicize the internal debates we had amongst the eleven judges who heard the matter. Confidentiality and collegiality are integral to the proper functioning of any Court. Nor would it be correct for me to seek to defend the decision, or even to outline the thought processes that went into it. The judgment is a public document with a public meaning. It must speak for itself, without subsequent gloss or explanatory notes by its author. What I can say, however, is that the finalization of the judgment took several months, and that it is the practice of the Court to workshop complex matters, sometimes three, four or five times, to ensure that the views of all colleagues are fully taken into account. The goal is to reach a principled consensus wherever possible. And I can offer some signposts to facilitate understanding of the main issues. At the end, the reader will be able to look through actual texts taken from the judgment, and make up his or her own mind whether my earlier experiences with the two different communities, found any echoes in what I came to write.

Readers of the judgment will note that it does not pick up on the controversies that surged from the way courts in Vermont, Massachusetts, Canada or the United Kingdom dealt with same-sex marriages. Polemics migrated from country to country, and the same arguments were sent on by the supporters of both sides. It was extremely helpful to read them, but in the end the complicated legal arguments they contained, based on different constitutional texts, were not rehearsed in our decision. Far more helpful was the rich store of South African legal materials on the significance of the equality in our Constitution forbidding unfair discrimination on the grounds of sexual orientation, and the manifestly diverse nature of family formations in our country.

Sexual Orientation

Establishing that there was unfair discrimination was relatively straightforward in the South African legal context. The Constitution identified sexual orientation as a forbidden ground of unfair discrimination—it was explicit. Our Court had dealt with five cases that had turned on that prohibition. In the first we struck down the crime of sodomy. The next, the *Home Affairs* case, dealt with the rights under immigration law of foreign same-sex partners in South Africa. Should these rights be the same as those enjoyed by foreign spouses—wives and husbands—of South Africans? Foreign spouses of South Africans received two benefits: they could work without a special permit, and they could come into the country and apply for resident status on South African soil. The Court declared that the failure of the Immigration Act to provide these benefits for same-sex partners amounted to unfair discrimination against them. Yet it would not have made sense to strike down manifestly beneficial provisions in the Act which permitted heterosexual people to marry. The fact was that the Act was unconstitutional not because of what it said, but because of what it left out—in legal language, it was under-inclusive. So to create equality, our Court for the first time read remedial provisions into the law, there and then. We added after the word 'spouses' in the Act the phrase 'or life partners in same-sex relationships'. Then the judgment gave something of a definition of what the phrase meant, and left it to Home Affairs to work out the practical implications.

We in a later case upheld Judge Kathy Satchwell's claim that her lesbian partner should be able to enjoy the same pension benefits that a married spouse would have enjoyed. In the next case the lesbian partner of a judge who had adopted twins sought equal parental rights in relation to the children, and we declared that being prevented from achieving this status under the Adoption Act was unconstitutional—not only did it represent unfair discrimination against her, but it also went against the best interests of the children. A similar decision followed concerning the parentage of a child born through *in vitro* fertilization.

The judgment I wrote refers to these cases. It also places considerable emphasis on the multiplicity of family formations in our country, where for a long period only the Christian marriage, clearly heterosexual in those days, was recognized. Thus Muslim marriages were not recognized because they were potentially polygamous, with the result that wives from England had a right to join their husbands, while wives from India did not. When Gandhi fought against that, and people voluntarily went to jail in protest, he spoke about our mothers and our sisters, as he put it, armed only with the patriotism of faith, making perhaps a greater sacrifice than did the men, going to jail because they were called concubines and their children designated as illegitimate. And African customary marriages, the most performed marriages in the country, were almost completely marginalized. And so the diversity of marriage formations, the way human beings lived together and expressed their intimacy and connected with the rest of society, features strongly in the judgment.

Source of the Discrimination

Granted, then, that our precedent and history showed that there was indeed unfair discrimination against same-sex couples, two further questions remained: what precisely was the source of the discrimination, and could the Court itself provide the remedy, or should the matter be referred to Parliament? And the arguments were basically two-fold: first, the Court can't itself do something so drastic, so intrusive on popular culture, so contrary to received practices and the laws of the centuries as to create the institution of same-sex marriage. Only Parliament could do so. The most the Court could do, it was contended, was to declare that there was a gap in the law, and then leave it to Parliament to provide the remedy. The subsidiary argument was as follows: even if same-sex couples should be able lawfully to regulate their relationships in respect of property, inheritance, tenancies, pensions and so on, this did not mean that their newly-recognized relationships should be referred to as marriages. To use the term marriage would be to fly in the face of biology, history, religion, and law.

The judgment structured itself around delineating the character of the unfair discrimination involved. It held that the unfairness flowed from not according to same-sex couples the same status, rights and responsibilities that the law accorded to heterosexual couples. The question of status was highlighted. Marriage involves both tangibles and intangibles. Marriages are celebrated, you have anniversaries and a huge part of our culture centres itself around marriage. To contend that acknowledgement of the love, the intimacy, and public recognition of the relationship between same-sex couples, would tarnish and demean the institution of marriage, was intensely repugnant to the dignity of same-sex couples.

A footnote in the judgment indicated that some radical queer literature said, in effect: 'We don't want to replicate heterosexual forms of relationships which have involved so much oppression to heterosexual couples, and which are so bound up with property relationships—that's not what we want.' But once the battle was joined, overwhelmingly the gay and lesbian literature argued for the right of same-sex couples to choose whether to marry or not. And because of the symbolism of marriage, the right of same-sex couple to choose whether to marry or not, became a touchstone, a symbol of achieving full legal recognition, a chance for joyous public celebration (and, maybe, for tearful divorce).

Once the character of the discrimination had been established it was necessary to decide on the question of remedy. Should the Court itself provide the remedy, or should it simply refer the matter to Parliament?

My colleague Kate O'Regan—who, incidentally had been educated at a convent—felt that the violation of fundamental rights was clear. It was accordingly the duty of the Court to develop the common law, which still followed the English law *Hyde v Hyde* definition (the union of one man and one woman for life). In her view, the Court should change the definition to bring it in line with the values of the Constitution. It would then read: marriage is the union of two people for life. She held further that we should follow the process we had followed in the *Home Affairs* case by reading in the gender-neutral word spouse into the Marriage Act ('Do you AB take CD to be your lawful husband/wife/*spouse?*'). If Parliament was dissatisfied with this formula it could amend the law as it saw fit, provided it respected the pronouncements of the Court on the constitutional issues involved. The remedy she proposed was simple, it could be done there and then, and had considerable precedent on its side. In her opinion, there was no need for the Court to delay the granting of rights by bringing Parliament into the picture.

Yet ten of us decided that Parliament should indeed be directly involved. Parliament had the same duty as the Court to uphold the Constitution. That's what the Members of Parliament swear they will do, whether they raise their right arms or affirm. The Bill of Rights had to be supported, protected, defended and advanced by all the branches of government, including Parliament, indeed, especially Parliament. Involving Parliament would ensure that it engaged with the population of South Africa, and so encourage the nation to get to grips with and face up to the issues involved. And so the decision that the majority of us took was that Parliament should be given one year to correct the defect. If it failed to do so, then we ordered that the words 'or spouse' would automatically be written into the Marriage Act.

The result was that Parliament was given the opportunity to decide not *whether*, but *how* the unfair discrimination should be overcome. The effect was to encourage Parliament to go out to the nation at public hearings and get a national dialogue going on the issue. And both when dealing with the nature of unfair discrimination and in its section on remedy, the judgment offered a certain number of clarifications and words of caution.

The Sacred and the Secular

One of the central preoccupations of the judgment was how to ensure that the sacred and the secular could co-exist in the same public realm. The answer it proposes is not to separate a secular public realm from a sacred private realm. It accepts, rather, that religion is part of public life, with intense meaning to millions of people who, incidentally, had been on all sides of the freedom struggle, and indeed, who differed amongst themselves on the question of same-sex marriages. The judgment makes it clear that the Marriage Act fully protects the rights of religious confessions and faiths and denominations to conduct their own marriage ceremonies according to their own tenets. Nothing in the judgment would compel them to celebrate marriages in a way that would violate their religious consciences. They were protected by the Marriage Act and by the Constitution—it was part of their rights to religious freedom. There might well be battles inside the different confessions as to what the true tenets of the religion were, but that was for the members of their religion to deal with, it was not for the State to tell them what to do.

The judgment underlines the fact that religion has to be taken seriously, and the beliefs of the people acknowledged and respected as part of the public realm. But the law had to acknowledge the undeniable, incontestable claims of gay and lesbian couples to celebrate in a public way, with the State's support and backing, their relationships, their intimacy, their love, their feelings for each other—that was their human right protected by the Constitution. And what was left to Parliament was simply to determine the modalities to enable them to enjoy their right to equality.

Equality of the Vineyard or the Graveyard?

The question then was how equality should be achieved. Should it be through achieving equality of the graveyard or equality of the vineyard?—terminology used by my colleague Laurie Ackermann in an earlier case on gay and lesbian rights, after he had picked it up from an American writer. Inequality can be eliminated either by levelling down (to the graveyard) or grading up (to the vineyard). American equal protection law is very much based on securing identical treatment for people in similar categories: in formal terms, levelling up and levelling down would each be consistent with the Constitution, and the author was trying to find a principled way of determining when equality should be achieved by levelling up, and when by levelling down. And he proposed that the determination should be based on the underlying constitutional principles involved: which way would best promote the constitutional principle at stake?

In the case of same-sex couples there was no express exclusion by the law, nor was there differential treatment. Same-sex couples were simply ignored. Thus, the Marriage Act didn't expressly say 'Gays and lesbians need not apply'. They could marry, in fact, if they married heterosexual partners! The problem with the law was that it was under-inclusive, that it didn't go far enough. Do you remedy this by striking down the whole of the Marriage Act? Can you imagine, the Constitutional Court of South Africa declaring marriage to be unlawful for all because gays and lesbians cannot marry? A proposal that had in fact been put forward by the South African Law Reform Commission at an earlier stage was to have civil unions available for everybody and leave marriage purely to the religious bodies. If you want to marry, go to the shul or the temple, the mosque, or the cathedral, and get married—the state would not be involved. The state's role would be restricted to simply providing a civil ceremony to celebrate a civil union. Logical though this proposal was, it gathered little support. How would gay and lesbian couples feel if just when they are poised to enter the portals of marriage, the institution is abolished? And how would heterosexual couples feel, knowing that marriage had always been possible in the past, but now because of these darned people with their lobby groups, they couldn't get married any more? There would be equality, but equality of resentment. Promoting respect for the Bill of Rights meant emancipation for everybody, not grievance on an equal basis. And it was important to emphasize that to get true equality meant achieving equality of the status, of the opportunities, of the things that society values; effectively, in this case, equality of the vineyard. One certainly did not want endless litigation over the constitutionality of the remedy chosen.

'Separate but Equal'

The other issue in terms of which some general guidance is offered in the judgment relates to the 'separate but equal' doctrine. We were urged in argument to follow the civil partnership approach of the United Kingdom, because it didn't use the word 'marriage'. It would mean that gay and lesbian couples could regulate their property arrangements, succession, tenancies— all these practical things. But it would not interfere with the institution of marriage as historically constituted, we were told. The fact is that the separate but equal doctrine has had a strong and dolorous history not only in the United States, but also in our country. There was an abysmal decision by our top court, the Appeal Court, in the 1930s, when people of Indian origin objected to being excluded from Post-Office counters where white people would queue. Three out of four judges could not see the problem: the applicants could be served just as well in the one queue as in the other. Only one judge, Gardiner, who had been educated at Oxford, where he had called himself a socialist, and who had gone on to author what became a leading textbook on criminal law, said 'It touches on the dignity of people to be excluded, it's not simply a question of functionality.'

Three decades later Oliver Tambo, who was then in legal partnership with Nelson Mandela, and who went on to become the Acting President of the ANC in exile, was instructed to address a Magistrate from the section of the Bar reserved for non-Europeans. He refused, the matter was stood down, and at the next hearing his clerk Godfrey Pitje also refused to move. (I learnt later that Tambo had had underground work to do and couldn't afford to go to jail at that stage, so his clerk had agreed to stand in.) The clerk was found guilty of contempt of court. The case eventually went to the Appeal Court, and the Chief Justice stated that the clerk could have addressed the Court as well from one section of the bar as from the other, and upheld the fine imposed.

Our history showed, then, that separation was invariably based on prejudice with a purpose of shunning the group to be segregated out. Parliament now had to be sensitive to this, and not provide a new form of exclusion masquerading as equal treatment.

In the event, the media of the world was able to report that South Africa's highest court had held that same-sex couples had the right to marry and had given Parliament one year to pass the necessary legislation. And for the second time in my life my photograph appeared in the New York Times—the first image had been of me recovering from the bomb in a London hospital, swathed in bandages, now it showed me in my green robes, flanked by law colleagues, with my law clerk sitting below (the picture appears at p vii).

Parliament duly set about holding public hearings. There were many vociferous attacks on the idea of same-sex marriages—and only a few people defended it. Acutely homophobic statements were recorded. But if we had homophobes in our society, it was better that they declared themselves publicly, than that the issues be disguised and never openly dealt with. After long deliberation, the South African Council of Churches issued a statement saying that they had studied the judgment, and praised it for its Solomonic approach, which particularly pleased me because my Dad's name happened to be Solomon (Solly Sachs).

The Involvement of Parliament

In any event we had given Parliament one year to correct the defect in the law. That is a power that the Constitution entrusts to the Court: you declare something to be unconstitutional, and suspend the declaration of invalidity to allow the law to be corrected. And we didn't want the Marriage Act, if it was not amended, to be invalidated for unconstitutionality after the year—that would have been a disastrous outcome. So we said if Parliament didn't correct the defect within the year, then the Marriage Act would automatically have read into it the phrase 'or spouse', which would correct the discrimination. That was the fallback position. And just a couple of days before the year was up, Parliament enacted what it called the Civil Union Act.

What distinguished it from the Civil Partnership Act in the United Kingdom lay not only in the use of the word 'union', but in permitting the declarants, who might be of the same sex, to say 'I enter into a civil union with you' or, if they prefer, 'I marry you'. The word 'marry' is used in that Act.

A caveat introduced into the judgment had been to the effect that Parliament could in the spirit of reasonable accommodation consider allowing Marriage Officers who had deep, genuine objections based on religious belief to marrying same-sex couples, not to be compelled to do so. This was incorporated into the law. To be married by someone whom you feel is loathing the process would mark a terrible beginning to a relationship. And as a matter of principle, the state should take reasonable measures wherever possible to avoid sincere religious believers from having to make extremely burdensome choices between obeying the law or following their consciences. What's important is for the State to employ people who are happy with the new constitutional values, and who can marry same-sex couples with love rather than with loathing in their hearts. And it has taken a little bit of time, but these Marriage Officers have been found, and they celebrate same-sex marriages in a very dignified way, as part of the law of the land.

I end with the reflection that Courts should seek wherever possible to engage with the whole nation. It's not for court judgments to divide the nation between progressives and reactionaries, liberals and conservatives, with the court opting to back one view or the other and intensifying those divisions, and with people then fighting bitterly over the court decisions. The courts should try to find a language in keeping with the Constitution that will make people say, 'I might not be at all happy with the outcome, but I can see what the Court is getting at, I was properly listened to, and maybe next time I will be on the winning side. At the end of the day I can see what it means to be a South African with rights in the new South Africa.'

A Coda, and a Coda to the Coda

And I end the end with a coda, and a further coda to the coda. In January, just a couple of weeks after the new law was adopted, I am driving to Kirstenbosch Botanical Gardens in Cape Town—beautiful gardens on the side of Table Mountain, the most family-oriented place you can imagine. I'm looking for where to go, and I see a sign, just a simple sign, that says 'To Amy and Jean's marriage'—the arrow goes that way. My heart just leaps, because it is so simple and so banal and so ordinary. And Jean who's a South African living in Washington with her American partner, Amy, tells us she had booked the place for the reception on the telephone—but had felt a few days before the event that she ought to tell the manageress that in fact they were two women, and the manageress had said 'How wonderful—you'll be the first, and I'm so happy that you chose us.'

The coda to the coda is that not too long afterwards the newspapers were filled with the news of the marriage of Zackie Achmat, prominent leader of the Treatment Action Campaign, a body that concerned itself with the treatment to be given to people living with HIV, and his partner of a couple of years, who happened to come from a rural Afrikaans-speaking white family from the Free State. Justice Edwin Cameron had arranged to be appointed a Marriage Officer just for the one day to officiate.

And everybody wanted to be invited to this celebrity-type wedding. It turned out that Zackie and his partner had told Edwin that they didn't want to use the word 'marriage'—such a heterosexist concept. And Edwin had apparently persuaded them that people had fought hard for the right to be married, and it would give a status and dignity to the relationship that the colder terminology of 'union' and 'partnership' just wouldn't have done. And so Zackie said 'I marry you' and his partner said 'I marry you'. The occasion entered the social pages, which discussed what people were wearing, and what the food was like, and the little speeches that were made. And most remarkable of all: the family of his partner, from one of the most socially conservative parts of the country, said that his father, no longer alive, would have been so proud of his son that day.

The *Fourie* Case

Extracts from the judgment I wrote, which was agreed to by all but one of my colleagues.

SACHS J:

[Equality across difference]

Equality means equal concern and respect across difference. It does not presuppose the elimination or suppression of difference. Respect for human rights requires the affirmation of self, not the denial of self. Equality therefore does not imply a levelling or homogenisation of behaviour or extolling one form as supreme, and another as inferior, but an acknowledgement and acceptance of difference. At the very least, it affirms that difference should not be the basis for exclusion, marginalisation and stigma. At best, it celebrates the vitality that difference brings to any society. The issue goes well beyond assumptions of heterosexual exclusivity, a source of contention in the present case. The acknowledgement and acceptance of difference is particularly important in our country where for centuries group membership based on supposed biological characteristics such as skin colour has been the express basis of advantage and disadvantage. South Africans come in all shapes and sizes. The Constitution thus acknowledges the variability of human beings (genetic and socio-cultural), affirms the right to be different, and celebrates the diversity of the nation. Accordingly, what is at stake is not simply a question of removing an injustice experienced by a particular section of the community. At issue is a need to affirm the very character of our society as one based on tolerance and mutual respect. The test of tolerance is not how one finds space for people with whom, and practices with which, one feels comfortable, but how one accommodates the expression of what is discomfiting.

[The antiquity of prejudice]

The exclusion of same-sex couples from the benefits and responsibilities of marriage, is not a small and tangential inconvenience resulting from a few surviving relics of societal prejudice destined to evaporate like the morning dew. It represents a harsh if oblique statement by the law that same-sex couples are outsiders, and that their need for affirmation and protection of their intimate relations as human beings is somehow less than that of heterosexual couples. It reinforces the wounding notion that they are to be treated as biological oddities, as failed or lapsed human beings who do not fit into normal society, and, as such, do not qualify for the full moral concern and respect that our Constitution seeks to secure for everyone. It signifies that their capacity for love, commitment and accepting responsibility is by definition less worthy of regard than that of heterosexual couples.

It follows that, given the centrality attributed to marriage and its consequences in our culture, to deny same-sex couples a choice in this respect is to negate their right to self-definition in a most profound way.

The antiquity of a prejudice is no reason for its survival. Slavery lasted for a century and a half in this country, colonialism for twice as long, the prohibition of interracial marriages for even longer, and overt male domination for millennia. All were based on apparently self-evident biological and social facts; all were once sanctioned by religion and imposed by law; the first two are today regarded with total disdain, and the third with varying degrees of denial, shame or embarrassment. Similarly, the fact that the law today embodies conventional majoritarian views in no way mitigates its discriminatory impact. It is precisely those groups that cannot count on popular support and strong representation in the legislature that have a claim to vindicate their fundamental rights through application of the Bill of Rights.

[The public meaning of religion]

In the open and democratic society contemplated by the Constitution, although the rights of non-believers and minority faiths must be fully respected, the religious beliefs held by the great majority of South Africans must be taken seriously. As this Court pointed out in *Christian Education*, freedom of religion goes beyond protecting the inviolability of the individual conscience. For many believers, their relationship with God or creation is central to all their activities. It concerns their capacity to relate in an intensely meaningful fashion to their sense of themselves, their community and their universe. For millions in all walks of life, religion provides support and nurture and a framework for individual and social stability and growth. Religious belief has the capacity to awaken concepts of self-worth and human dignity which form the cornerstone of human rights. Such belief affects the believer's view of society and founds a distinction between right and wrong. It expresses itself in the affirmation and continuity of powerful traditions that frequently have an ancient character transcending historical epochs and national boundaries. For believers, then, what is at stake is not merely a question of convenience or comfort, but an intensely held sense about what constitutes the good and proper life and their place in creation.

Religious bodies play a large and important part in public life, through schools, hospitals and poverty relief programmes. They command ethical behaviour from their members and bear witness to the exercise of power by state and private agencies; they promote music, art and theatre; they provide halls for community activities, and conduct a great variety of social activities for their members and the general public. They are part of the fabric of public life, and constitute active elements of the diverse and pluralistic nation contemplated by the Constitution. Religion is not just a question of belief or doctrine. It is part of a people's temper and culture, and for many believers a significant part of their way of life. Religious organisations constitute important sectors of national life and accordingly have a right to express themselves to government and the courts on the great issues of the day. They are active participants in public affairs fully entitled to have their say with regard to the way law is made and applied.

Furthermore, in relation to the extensive national debates concerning rights for homosexuals, it needs to be acknowledged that though religious strife may have produced its own forms of intolerance, and religion may have been used in this country to justify the most egregious forms of racial discrimination, it would be wrong and unhelpful to dismiss opposition to homosexuality on religious grounds simply as an expression of bigotry to be equated to racism. As Ackermann J said in the *Sodomy* case:

> The issues in this case touch on deep convictions and evoke strong emotions. It must not be thought that the view which holds that sexual expression should be limited to marriage

between men and women with procreation as its dominant or sole purpose, is held by crude bigots only. On the contrary, it is also sincerely held, for considered and nuanced religious and other reasons, by persons who would not wish to have the physical expression of sexual orientation differing from their own proscribed by the law.

It is also necessary, however, to highlight his qualification:

It is nevertheless equally important to point out that such views, however honestly and sincerely held, cannot influence what the Constitution dictates in regard to discrimination on the grounds of sexual orientation.

[The sacred and the secular]

It is one thing for the Court to acknowledge the important role that religion plays in our public life. It is quite another to use religious doctrine as a source for interpreting the Constitution. It would be out of order to employ the religious sentiments of some as a guide to the constitutional rights of others. Between and within religions there are vastly different and at times highly disputed views on how to respond to the fact that members of their congregations and clergy are themselves homosexual. Judges would be placed in an intolerable situation if they were called upon to construe religious texts and take sides on issues which have caused deep schisms within religious bodies.

One respects the sincerity with which Mr. Smyth cited passages in the Old and New Testaments in support of his argument that what he referred to as a change in the definition of marriage would discriminate against persons who believed that marriage was a heterosexual institution ordained of God, and who regarded their marriage vows as sacred. Yet for the purpose of legal analysis, such appreciation would not imply accepting that those sources may appropriately be relied upon by a court. Whether or not the Biblical texts support his beliefs would certainly not be a question which this Court could entertain. From a constitutional point of view, what matters is for the Court to ensure that he be protected in his right to regard his marriage as sacramental, to belong to a religious community that celebrates its marriages according to its own doctrinal tenets, and to be free to express his views in an appropriate manner both in public and in Court. Further than that the Court could not be expected to go.

In the open and democratic society contemplated by the Constitution there must be mutually respectful co-existence between the secular and the sacred. The function of the Court is to recognise the sphere which each inhabits, not to force the one into the sphere of the other. Provided there is no prejudice to the fundamental rights of any person or group, the law will legitimately acknowledge a diversity of strongly-held opinions on matters of great public controversy. I stress the qualification that there must be no prejudice to basic rights. Majoritarian opinion can often be harsh to minorities that exist outside the mainstream. It is precisely the function of the Constitution and the law to step in and counteract rather than reinforce unfair discrimination against a minority. The test, whether majoritarian or minoritarian positions are involved, must always be whether the measure under scrutiny promotes or retards the achievement of human dignity, equality and freedom.

The hallmark of an open and democratic society is its capacity to accommodate and manage difference of intensely-held world views and lifestyles in a reasonable and fair manner. The objective of the Constitution is to allow different concepts about the nature of human existence to inhabit the same public realm, and to do so in a manner that is not mutually destructive and that at the same time enables government to function in a way that shows equal concern and respect for all.

The need for co-existence and respect for diversity of belief is in fact expressly recognised by the Marriage Act. The Act in terms permits religious leaders to be designated as marriage officers, religious buildings to be used for the solemnisation of marriages, the marriage formula usually observed by a religious denomination to be employed and its religious marriage rites to be followed. It is not only permissible to solemnise marriages in these ways. All such marriages are recognised and given legal force by the state. Legal consequences flow from them as from a civil marriage celebrated before a magistrate or other state marriage officer. The state interest in marriage ceremonies performed by religious leaders is protected by empowering the Minister of Home Affairs to designate the ministers of religion concerned and to approve of the marriage formula being followed.

No minister of religion could be compelled to solemnise a same-sex marriage if such a marriage would not conform to the doctrines of the religion concerned. There is nothing in the matters before us that either directly or indirectly trenches in any way on this strong protection of the right of religious communities not to be obliged to celebrate marriages not conforming to their tenets.

It is clear from the above that acknowledgement by the state of the right of same-sex couples to enjoy the same status, entitlements and responsibilities as marriage law accords to heterosexual couples is in no way inconsistent with the rights of religious organisations to continue to refuse to celebrate same-sex marriages. The constitutional claims of same-sex couples can accordingly not be negated by invoking the rights of believers to have their religious freedom respected. The two sets of interests involved do not collide, they co-exist in a constitutional realm based on accommodation of diversity.

[The role of Parliament]

It is clear that just as the Marriage Act denies equal protection and subjects same-sex couples to unfair discrimination by excluding them from its ambit, so and to the same extent does the common law definition of marriage fall short of constitutional requirements. It is necessary, therefore, to make a declaration to the effect that the common law definition of marriage is inconsistent with the Constitution and invalid to the extent that it fails to provide to same-sex couples the status and benefits coupled with responsibilities which it accords to heterosexual couples. The question then arises whether, having made such declaration, the Court itself should develop the common law so as to remedy the consequences of the common law's under-inclusive character.

[*The judgment states that inclusion of the word 'or spouse' in the Marriage Act would automatically override the common law definition of marriage.*] Thus corrected, the Marriage Act would then have to be interpreted and applied in a manner consistent with the constitutional requirement that same-sex couples be treated with the same concern and respect as that accorded to heterosexual couples. The effect would be that formal registration of same-sex unions would automatically extend the common law and statutory legal consequences to same-sex couples that flow to heterosexual couples from marriage...

The question that arises is whether this Court is obliged to provide immediate relief in the terms sought by the applicants and the Equality Project, or whether it should suspend the order of invalidity to give Parliament a chance to remedy the defect. The test is what is just and equitable, taking account of all the circumstances...

This is a matter involving status that requires a remedy that is secure. To achieve security it needs to be firmly located within the broad context of an extended search for emancipation of a section of society that has known protracted and bitter oppression. The circumstances of the present matter call out for enduring and stable legislative appreciation. A temporary remedial measure would be far less likely to achieve the enjoyment of equality as promised by the Constitution than would lasting legislative action compliant with the Constitution.

The claim by the applicants in *Fourie* of the right to get married should, in my view, be seen as part of a comprehensive wish to be able to live openly and freely as lesbian women emancipated from all the legal taboos that historically have kept them from enjoying life in the mainstream of society. The right to celebrate their union accordingly signifies far more than a right to enter into a legal arrangement with many attendant and significant consequences, important though they may be. It represents a major symbolical milestone in their long walk to equality and dignity. The greater and more secure the institutional imprimatur for their union, the more solidly will it and other such unions be rescued from legal oblivion, and the more tranquil and enduring will such unions ultimately turn out to be.

This is a matter that touches on deep public and private sensibilities. I believe that Parliament is well-suited to finding the best ways of ensuring that same-sex couples are brought in from the legal cold. The law may not automatically and of itself eliminate stereotyping and prejudice. Yet it serves as a great teacher, establishes public norms that become assimilated into daily life and protects vulnerable people from unjust marginalisation and abuse. It needs to be remembered that not only the courts are responsible for vindicating the rights enshrined in the Bill of Rights. The legislature is in the frontline in this respect. One of its principal functions is to ensure that the values of the Constitution as set out in the Preamble and section 1 permeate every area of the law.

This judgment serves to vindicate the rights of the applicants by declaring the manner in which the law at present fails to meet their equality claims. At the same time, it is my view that it would best serve those equality claims by respecting the separation of powers and giving Parliament an opportunity to deal appropriately with the matter. In this respect it is necessary to bear in mind that there are different ways in which the legislature could legitimately deal with the gap that exists in the law...

Given the great public significance of the matter, the deep sensitivities involved and the importance of establishing a firmly-anchored foundation for the achievement of equality in this area, it is appropriate that the legislature be given an opportunity to map out what it considers to be the best way forward. The one unshakeable criterion is that the present exclusion of same-sex couples from enjoying the status and entitlements coupled with the responsibilities that are accorded to heterosexual couples by the common law and the Marriage Act, is constitutionally unsustainable. The defect must be remedied so as to ensure that same-sex couples are not subjected to marginalisation or exclusion by the law, either directly or indirectly...

In exercising its legislative discretion Parliament will have to bear in mind that the objective of the new measure must be to promote human dignity, the achievement of equality and the advancement of human rights and freedoms. This means in the first place taking account of the fact that in overcoming the under-inclusiveness of the common law and the Marriage Act, it would be inappropriate to employ a remedy that created equal disadvantage for all. Thus the achievement of equality would not be accomplished by ensuring that if same-sex couples cannot enjoy the status and entitlements coupled with the responsibilities of marriage, the same should apply to heterosexual couples. Levelling down so as to deny access to civil marriage to all would not promote the achievement of the enjoyment of equality. Such parity of exclusion rather than of inclusion would distribute resentment evenly, instead of dissipating it equally for all. The law concerned with family formation and marriage requires equal celebration, not equal marginalisation; it calls for equality of the vineyard and not equality of the graveyard...

Whatever legislative remedy is chosen must be as generous and accepting towards same-sex couples as it is to heterosexual couples, both in terms of the intangibles as well as the tangibles involved.

[Ending the isolation of same-sex couples]
Lying at the heart of this case is a wish to bring to an end, or at least diminish, the isolation to which the law has long subjected same-sex couples. It is precisely because marriage plays such a profound role in terms of the way our society regards

itself, that the exclusion from the common law and Marriage Act of same-sex couples is so injurious, and that the foundation for the construction of new paradigms needs to be steadily and securely laid. It is appropriate that Parliament be given a free hand, within the framework established by this judgment, to shoulder its responsibilities in this respect...

[*The judgment states that if Parliament fails to provide an appropriate remedy within twelve months, the words 'or spouse' will automatically be read into the Marriage Act, enabling same-sex couples to marry.*]

Reading-in of the words 'or spouse' has the advantage of being simple and direct. It involves minimal textual alteration. The values of the Constitution would be upheld. The existing institutional mechanisms for the celebration of marriage would remain the same. Budgetary implications would be minimal. The long-standing policy of the law to protect and enhance family life would be sustained and extended. Negative stereotypes would be undermined. Religious institutions would remain undisturbed in their ability to perform marriage ceremonies according to their own tenets, and thus if they wished, to celebrate heterosexual marriages only. The principle of reasonable accommodation could be applied by the state to ensure that civil marriage officers who had sincere religious objections to officiating at same-sex marriages would not themselves be obliged to do so if this resulted in a violation of their conscience.

Justice Kate O'Reagan agreed with the main body of the judgment, but wrote a short dissent on the question of remedy. In her view the Court itself should change the common-law definition of marriage and insert the gender-neutral word 'or spouse' into the Marriage Act with immediate effect, and not send the matter to Parliament, with a year's delay.

O'REAGAN J:

The power and duty to protect constitutional rights is conferred upon the courts and courts should not shrink from that duty. The legitimacy of an order made by the Court does not flow from the status of the institution itself, but from the fact that it gives effect to the provisions of our Constitution. Time and again, there will be those in our broader community who do not wish to see constitutional rights protected, but that can never be a reason for a court not to protect those rights.

10

The Beginning and the End

In the beginning and in the end is the word, at least as far as the life of a judge is concerned. We pronounce. We work with words, and become amongst the most influential story-tellers of our age. How we tell the story is often as important as what we say. The voice we use cannot be that of a depersonalized and divine oracle that declares solutions to the problems of human life through the enunciation of pure and detached wisdom. Nor dare we seek to imitate the artificial sound of a computer that has been programmed to produce inexorable outcomes. We speak with the living voices of real protagonists who are immersed in and affected by the very processes we deal with. If law is a machine we are the ghosts that inhabit it and give it life. We are animated by consciences that will have been shaped not only by our learning but by our varied engagements with life, by experiences both inside and outside the law. And we continue to live in the very world on which we pronounce. Indeed, being a judge and participating in the work of the courts is nothing less than a rich and ongoing life experience in itself.

We discover that a collegial court is more than the sum of its parts. It has its own vitality, its own dynamic, its own culture. We subsume ourselves into it. We do not seek to escape from the precedential narcissism that lies at the self-referential heart of the judicial function. We glory in it, and in a studied and self-conscious manner expose ourselves to the world as exemplars of people who live not by the sword or the purse but by provisioning reasons. As I have sought to show, giving reasons for what we do is not the same as engaging in pure reasoning. Though the use of hard logic is part of the reasoning process, it is only a part. Good and convincing legal reasoning will inevitably be informed by experience and derive its vitality and sustainability from its congruence with life.

Psychologists, sociologists and political scientists might offer good explanations for why judges make particular decisions, yet the furnishing of explanations of judicial conduct cannot be equated with the giving of reasons for judicial decisions.

I might have an abhorrence for corporal punishment because I was frequently and unjustly caned at school, or heard the cries of juveniles being whipped in the jail where I was locked up. This could explain why I had an innate sensitivity to the question of corporal punishment. Yet the early experiences in my life did not dictate the outcome of a judgment I came to write involving a claim by Christian Education Schools of their right as part of their religion to use corporal correction in their particular schools, even though it had been prohibited in schools generally. Why was I not amongst the men who thought that having been beaten at school strengthened their character? And how had my abhorrence for caning to be balanced against another deep experience I had had at school, namely, that of seeking to protect the integrity of my right as a person of conscience not to pretend adherence to a religious belief that I did not possess?

By the time I came to be a judge, the raw energy of these diverse experiences had been transmuted by multiple other life experiences and kneaded by innumerable reflections at different stages of my life to become part of a complex and ever evolving legal world-view. The beauty and terror of legal concepts is that they are at the same time both completely abstract and totally immersed in real life situations. So in setting out the judgment, having veered this way and that on the journey to write it up, I felt it necessary to explain the issues not in terms of my particular experiences but in relation to the constitutional values involved. These values had been drawn from life experiences of millions over the ages. They reconciled the passion in the law of which Justice Brennan spoke, with the prescriptive quality of all legal norms. What the judgment required, however, was not a philosophical treatise on the right to bodily integrity versus the right to freedom of conscience, but a carefully thought-through balancing of the way these two rights interconnected in the concrete circumstances of the case. And all readers, especially the litigants, had to be apprised of the factors that had influenced my decision, in particular why I had felt the balance came out in a particular way. The broad philosophical conclusion to which I came has been set out in *Religious Exemption from General Law* (see Chapter 4, p 123) and need not be repeated. The ruling of the Court was in fact that, the subject to common law principles governing reasonable chastisement, the Christian Education community could maintain the integrity of their faith at home but not impose corporal correction in the more public environ of the schools. I like to think that disappointed as they might have been by the result, the Schools felt that the depth of their convictions had been appreciated and taken seriously, and that they and anyone reading the judgment would know exactly what proportionate weight had been given to the different objective considerations that had played a part in determining the outcome.

Looking back on my years on the Bench, then, I have no doubt that life experiences have entered into my legal consciousness in multiple ways, some very obvious and others quite mysterious. All have been integrated into and transformed by the legal culture in which my Court has operated. The little that I can say with confidence is that our task has not been simply to try to solve problems through formal legal reasoning. Nor, on the other hand, has it merely been to wrap up purely personal preferences in legal vocabulary. Our judicial function has been to identify issues, to weigh the different considerations involved, to arrive at a proportionately balanced outcome that took account of the context and the constitutional values at stake and to share with the public all the reasoning that led to the final product. In a word, it has been to judge.

Epilogue and Thanks

I was 73 years old and quietly putting finishing touches to this manuscript while on long leave as a Ford Foundation Scholar in Residence, when I discovered I was a counter-revolutionary. Why? Because I was a member of the Constitutional Court. According to a senior official of the ANC the Court was part of a group of counter-revolutionary forces trying to stop the President of the ANC, Jacob Zuma, from becoming President of the country. Happily, a few weeks later in response to an outcry that followed the remarks, the official stated he had been quoted out of context, and the ANC re-affirmed its support for the Constitution and the independence of the judiciary. So I write this epilogue knowing that, for some months at least, I have not been a counter-revolutionary.

Meanwhile news came through that Mrs Grootboom had died, never having moved from her shack to a brick house. The government praised her posthumously for her work as a fighter for the homeless. There were countless newspaper editorials that paid tribute to her. Yet the fact that her family were not yet housed in reasonable accommodation showed how difficult it was to realise the socio-economic rights in the Constitution.

The years on the Court have not always been free from moments of pain and discomfort. At troubled moments I often think of the calm and thoughtful way in which Oliver Tambo, after whom our child was named, managed to maintain his intellectual and spiritual poise. But overwhelmingly my years as a judge have been intense, productive, and joyous. When writing this book I wished I could have spoken about the wonderful debates we had around the conference table, and longed to describe the multiple metamorphoses that judgments underwent before being finally delivered. Yet I could not violate the confidentiality which lies at the heart of our collegial enterprise. The only way I felt I could appropriately sustain the internal dynamic of the book was to insert material largely from my own judgments. In this manner I could say something about the tocks and ticks of my own mind without betraying any inter-collegial confidence.

Yet even within this limited frame, I was nervous. Was I breaking some unofficial judicial taboo? To test the waters, I sent the manuscript to a number of judges. And to my surprise (mingled with satisfaction) I discovered that overwhelmingly they expressed appreciation, even enthusiasm.

Richard Goldstone, who had been on the Court with me for a number of years, immediately gave me the reassurance that in his view there was nothing in the book that was out of line. That was a relief. Then followed very supportive comments from Justices Frank North in Australia, Rosalie Abella and Clare L'Heureux Dube in Canada, and Wilhelmina Thomassen of the Netherlands. Later, I sent copies to Justices I had met at a lunch at the United States Supreme Court. Justice Antonin Scalia responded quickly and graciously, saying that I had accurately represented his viewpoints (which happened to be diametrically opposed to my own), demurring only in relation to my comment that he was as amiable off the bench as he could be severe when on it. Justice Ruth Bader Ginsburg spent hours with the manuscript and produced a precise and extremely helpful critique. She also referred me to a book and a recent article in the New Yorker, which together showed that there were people in many occupations who had had moments of unbidden discovery remarkably similar to my epiphanies in the bath. (A psychotherapist friend told me about the three places-of-discovery—Bed, Bath and Bus.)

Writing is lonely, hard and ennervating. When a person spontaneously picks up some of the surrounding burdens, the emotion of gratitude is particularly strong. Sarah Hibbin, of the School of Oriental and African Studies in London, not only made immediate contact with Oxford University Press, but also sent the manuscript on to a number of senior judges I knew in the UK. It might be that some of the recipients thought it kinder not to reply at all, but those who did write back, could not have been more supportive. I was particularly buoyed by comments I received from former Lord Chief Justice Harry Woolf, and Law Lords Tom Bingham and Robert Walker. I also had a most interesting discussion with Lord Justice Stephen Sedley who queried the appropriateness of appending one's own judgments to one's legal writings. He is a great legal stylist himself, and I hope I persuaded him that it depends on the nature of the book. And Lady Brenda Hale did not need to draw on all her considerable persuasive powers to get me to tone down the statement that every judgment I wrote was a lie.

A number of legal academics also made valuable inputs. Ursula Bentele of the Brooklyn Law School helped me with the very first draft of the very first chapters. Not only did she give me confidence at a time when I felt particularly unsure, she also saved me from the solecism of attributing the phrase 'confusion worse confounded' to Shakespeare rather than to Milton. Then there were two people who made particularly important chapter-by-chapter observations. One was a reader from Oxford University Press, clearly an academic, who remained anonymous—I cannot resist saying I will deal with Anon anon. So, first, let me thank Stephen Schulhofer of New York University, who simply as a friend engaged in a most stimulating and focussed way with both the substance and style of the book. That said, a special word of thanks to Anon. I just could not establish Anon's identity from the nature of the comments made and the language used, but whoever the person was, he or she captured the heart of what I was trying to do, and then challenged me with the most lively and helpful suggestions. Virtually all have been incorporated in the book.

Other contacts were more serendipitous. When I got an honorary degree at the University of Ulster, Christine Bell gave the oration, and in exchange received a copy of the manuscript. She went on to become the first person to use the text in class, and as a result of her interaction with the students, persuaded me to amplify the treatment on human dignity and proportionality. John Comaroff of Chicago University made valuable comments on the structure of the argument, some of which were quite radical and will have to await a possible separate publication. Jose Zalaquet of the University of Chile, who had asked me for a contribution to a human rights dictionary he was editing, received the entry plus the manuscript. He had advised us on setting up our Truth Commission and his comments on the chapter 'A Man Called Henri', were particularly valuable. Olga Khazova of the University of Moscow tested sections of the book on her son, with a positive response, she reported. The modest structural proposals she made, have, I think, rendered the book considerably more accessible.

There were other lawyers from different countries with different legal systems who also gave me the benefit of their responses. Dominique Remy-Granger, who formerly worked in the Conseil Constitutionel in Paris, made a number of astute observations and informed me that the first legal proclamation of socio-economic rights was not made in Prussia under Bismarck, as I had thought, but in France after the 1848 revolution. Then, after the draft chapter on 'Terrorism and Torture' had been circulated to the delegates at an International Bar Association conference in Buenos Aires, one of my hosts, Emilio Cardenas, asked to see the whole manuscript. Later he not only gave me insightful comments, he offered to translate the book into Spanish. Carol Steinberg sent me most helpful comments from Johannesburg. And to add to the diversity of localities, acute observations came from a Buddhist monastery in England, from where my friend Louise Stack occasionally sends me e-mails.

Two people in New York gave me encouragement without even realizing they were doing so. Dedi Felman, who had edited a book for a friend of mine, told me candidly that it would be difficult to find a United States publisher for a book about technical legal questions in a faraway country. This was at an early stage. Her words provoked me; and pique has its place in literary production. I felt there was a broader theme that went well beyond merely narrating parochial experiences of a South African judge. Audiences throughout the world had responded with great interest to presentations I had made. Her words pushed me to start exploring what the factors were that universally affected the way in which judges thought and functioned. And as I did so, the words, 'strange alchemy' kept coming to mind. And a whole new book emerged.

The other person who helped me was a babysitter. When I returned home one evening with my long-time cohabitant, now my marvellous wife Vanessa September, both of us bubbling with the music of *South Pacific*, the babysitter told me she had found the manuscript lying on a table, and was sorry that she had only managed to get half-way through before we got back. I knew then that the book had a future.

Finally, my assistant Marjorie Johnson in New York, and my law clerks, Kim Williams, Clare Ballard and Emmanuel de Groof in Johannesburg, have spent endless hours tirelessly working on endless revisions. To all of them I can now say: my deepest thanks, the alchemy has done its work—it is over, it really *is* over!

As I write these last words, the manuscript is being alchemized into a book under the steady and imaginative care of Alex Flach and with the gentle and sympathetic touch of Bethan Cousins. And to all the thankees, I offer a last post-final observation. Though I cannot absolve you from any errors, since I do not know what they might be, I can wholeheartedly say how much I appreciate your collegiality and assistance. At midnight on 12 October 2009 my fifteen-year term on the Court will expire. Whatever happens to this book, and whatever the destiny of my Court, you will have helped me to find my own personal manner to pay tribute to a remarkable phenomenon. In what seemed to many to be the most inhospitable terrain for constitutional justice in the world, the most advanced ideas on human dignity, equality and freedom have robustly, and I hope enduringly, taken root.

Appendix 1

The Constitution of the Republic of South Africa, 1996

Note that only those sections of the Constitution that are relevant to the discussion in this book are reproduced here.

Preamble

We, the people of South Africa,
Recognise the injustices of our past;
Honour those who suffered for justice and freedom in our land;
Respect those who have worked to build and develop our country; and
Believe that South Africa belongs to all who live in it, united in our diversity.
We therefore, through our freely elected representatives, adopt this Constitution as the supreme law of the Republic so as to—

- Heal the divisions of the past and establish a society based on democratic values, social justice and fundamental human rights;
- Lay the foundations for a democratic and open society in which government is based on the will of the people and every citizen is equally protected by law;
- Improve the quality of life of all citizens and free the potential of each person; and
- Build a united and democratic South Africa able to take its rightful place as a sovereign state in the family of nations.

May God protect our people.
Nkosi Sikelel' iAfrika. Morena boloka setjhaba sa heso.
God seën Suid-Afrika. God bless South Africa.
Mudzimu fhatutshedza Afurika. Hosi katekisa Afrika.

Founding Provisions

1. *Republic of South Africa*

The Republic of South Africa is one, sovereign, democratic state founded on the following values:

    a. Human dignity, the achievement of equality and the advancement of human rights and freedoms.

    b. Non-racialism and non-sexism.

    c. Supremacy of the constitution and the rule of law.

    d. Universal adult suffrage, a national common voters roll, regular elections and a multi-party system of democratic government, to ensure accountability, responsiveness and openness.

2. *Supremacy of Constitution*

This Constitution is the supreme law of the Republic; law or conduct inconsistent with it is invalid, and the obligations imposed by it must be fulfilled.

[...]

BILL OF RIGHTS

7. *Rights*

    1. This Bill of Rights is a cornerstone of democracy in South Africa. It enshrines the rights of all people in our country and affirms the democratic values of human dignity, equality and freedom.

    2. The state must respect, protect, promote and fulfil the rights in the Bill of Rights.

    3. The rights in the Bill of Rights are subject to the limitations contained or referred to in section 36, or elsewhere in the Bill.

[...]

9. *Equality*

    1. Everyone is equal before the law and has the right to equal protection and benefit of the law.

2. Equality includes the full and equal enjoyment of all rights and freedoms. To promote the achievement of equality, legislative and other measures designed to protect or advance persons, or categories of persons, disadvantaged by unfair discrimination may be taken.

3. The state may not unfairly discriminate directly or indirectly against anyone on one or more grounds, including race, gender, sex, pregnancy, marital status, ethnic or social origin, colour, sexual orientation, age, disability, religion, conscience, belief, culture, language and birth.

4. No person may unfairly discriminate directly or indirectly against anyone on one or more grounds in terms of subsection (3). National legislation must be enacted to prevent or prohibit unfair discrimination.

5. Discrimination on one or more of the grounds listed in subsection (3) is unfair unless it is established that the discrimination is fair.

10. *Human dignity*

Everyone has inherent dignity and the right to have their dignity respected and protected.

11. *Life*

Everyone has the right to life.

12. *Freedom and security of the person*

1. Everyone has the right to freedom and security of the person, which includes the right—
   a. not to be deprived of freedom arbitrarily or without just cause;
   b. not to be detained without trial;
   c. to be free from all forms of violence from either public or private sources;
   d. not to be tortured in any way; and
   e. not to be treated or punished in a cruel, inhuman or degrading way.
2. Everyone has the right to bodily and psychological integrity, which includes the right—

    a. to make decisions concerning reproduction;
    b. to security in and control over their body; and
    c. not to be subjected to medical or scientific experiments
       without their informed consent.

[…]

14. *Privacy*

Everyone has the right to privacy, which includes the right not to have—

    a. their person or home searched;
    b. their property searched;
    c. their possessions seized; or
    d. the privacy of their communications infringed.

15. *Freedom of religion, belief and opinion*

1. Everyone has the right to freedom of conscience, religion, thought, belief and opinion.
2. Religious observances may be conducted at state or state-aided institutions, provided that—

    a. those observances follow rules made by the appropriate public authorities;
    b. they are conducted on an equitable basis; and
    c. attendance at them is free and voluntary.

[…]

19. *Political rights*

[…]

3. Every adult citizen has the right—

    a. to vote in elections for any legislative body established in terms of the Constitution, and to do so in secret;

    […]

[…]

26. *Housing*

1. Everyone has the right to have access to adequate housing.
2. The state must take reasonable legislative and other measures, within its available resources, to achieve the progressive realisation of this right.

3. No one may be evicted from their home, or have their home demolished, without an order of court made after considering all the relevant circumstances. No legislation may permit arbitrary evictions.

27. *Health care, food, water and social security*

   1. Everyone has the right to have access to—

      a. health care services, including reproductive health care;

   [...]

   2. The state must take reasonable legislative and other measures, within its available resources, to achieve the progressive realisation of each of these rights.

   3. No one may be refused emergency medical treatment.

28. *Children*

   1. Every child has the right—

   [...]

      b. to family care or parental care, or to appropriate alternative care when removed from the family environment;

   [...]

   2. A child's best interests are of paramount importance in every matter concerning the child.

   3. In this section 'child' means a person under the age of 18 years.

   [...]

31. *Cultural, religious and linguistic communities*

   1. Persons belonging to a cultural, religious or linguistic community may not be denied the right, with other members of that community—

      a. to enjoy their culture, practise their religion and use their language; and

      b. to form, join and maintain cultural, religious and linguistic associations and other organs of civil society.

   2. The rights in subsection (1) may not be exercised in a manner inconsistent with any provision of the Bill of Rights.

   [...]

35. *Arrested, detained and accused persons*

[...]

> 3. Every accused person has a right to a fair trial, which includes the right—
>
> [...]
>
> h. to be presumed innocent, to remain silent, and not to testify during the proceedings;
>
> [...]

[...]

36. *Limitation of rights*

> 1. The rights in the Bill of Rights may be limited only in terms of law of general application to the extent that the limitation is reasonable and justifiable in an open and democratic society based on human dignity, equality and freedom, taking into account all relevant factors, including—
> a. the nature of the right;
> b. the importance of the purpose of the limitation;
> c. the nature and extent of the limitation;
> d. the relation between the limitation and its purpose; and
> e. less restrictive means to achieve the purpose.

[...]

38. *Interpretation of Bill of Rights*

> 1. When interpreting the Bill of Rights, a court, tribunal or forum—
> a. must promote the values that underlie an open and democratic society based on human dignity, equality and freedom;
> b. must consider international law; and
> c. may consider foreign law.
> 2. When interpreting any legislation, and when developing the common law or customary law, every court, tribunal or forum must promote the spirit, purport and objects of the Bill of Rights.

[...]

Appendix 2

South African Cases and Cases in Other Courts

All the South African cases referred to can be found on the Constitutional Court website <http://www.constitutionalcourt.org.za>. They are also reported in the South African Law Reports and the Butterworths Constitutional Law Reports, as cited below.

August and Another v Electoral Commission and Others 1999 (3) SA 1 CC; 1999 (4) BCLR 363 CC

Azanian People's Organisation (AZAPO) and Others v President of the Republic of South Africa and Others 1996 (4) SA 672 CC; 1996 (8) BCLR 1015 CC

Christian Education South Africa v Minister of Education 2000 (4) SA 757 (CC); 2000 (10) BCLR 1051 (CC)

Daniels v Campbell and Others 2004 (5) SA 331 (CC); 2004 (7) BCLR 735 (CC)

Dikoko v Mokhatla 2006 (6) SA 235 (CC); 2007(1) BCLR 1 (CC)

Government of the Republic of South Africa and Others v Grootboom and Others 2001 (1) SA 46 (CC); 2000 (11) BCLR 1169 (CC)

Hoffmann v South African Airways 2001 (1) SA 1 (CC); 2000 (11) BCLR 1235 (CC)

Kaunda and Others v President of the Republic of South Africa 2005 (4) SA 235 (CC); 2004 (10) BCLR 1009 (CC)

Laugh It Off Promotions CC v South African Breweries International (Finance) BV t/a Sabmark International and Another 2006 (1) SA 144 (CC); 2005 (8) BCLR 743 (CC)

Masetlha v President of the Republic of South Africa and Another 2008 (1) SA 556 (CC); 2008 (1) BLCR 1 (CC)

MEC for Health, KwaZulu-Natal v Premier, Kwazulu-Natal: In re Minister of Health and Others v Treatment Action Campaign and Others 2002 (5) SA 717 (CC); 2002 (10) BCLR 1028

Minister of Finance and Other v F J van Heerden 2004 (6) SA 121 (CC); 2004 (11) BCLR 1125 (CC)

Minister of Home Affairs and Another v Fourie and Another 2006 (1) SA 542 (CC); 2006 (3) BCLR 355 (CC)

Mohamed and Another v President of the Republic of South Africa and Others 2001 (3) SA 893 (CC); 2001 (7) BCLR 685 (CC)

Port Elizabeth Municipality v Various Occupiers 2005 (1) SA 217 (CC); 2004 (12) BCLR 1268 (CC)

Pretoria City Council v Walker 1998 (2) SA 363 (CC); 1998 (3) BCLR 257 (CC)

Prince v President of the Law Society of the Cape of Good Hope 2002 (2) SA 794 (CC); 2002 (3) BCLR 231 (CC)

S v Basson 2007 (3) SA 582 (CC); 2005 (12) BCLR 1192 (CC)

S v Coetzee and Others 1997 (3) SA 527 (CC); 1997 (4) BCLR 437(CC)

S v Jordan and Others (Sex Workers Education and Advocacy Task Force and Others as Amici Curiae 2002 (6) SA 642 (CC); 2002 (11) BCLR 1117 (CC)

S v Lawrence; S v Negal; S v Solberg 1997 (4) SA 1176 (CC); 1997 (10) BCLR 1348 (CC)

S v M 2008 (3) SA 232 (CC); 2007 (12) BCLR 1312 (CC)

S v Makwanyane and Another 1995 (3) SA 391 (CC); 1995 (6) BCLR 665 (CC)

Sidumo and Another v Rustenburg Platinum Mines Ltd and Others 2008 (2) SA 24 (CC); 2008 (2) BCLR 158 (CC)

Soobramoney v Minister of Health (Kwazulu-Natal) 1998 (1) SA 765 (CC); 1997 (12) BCLR 1696 (CC)

Volks v Robinson and Others 2005 (5) BCLR 446 (CC)

CASES IN OTHER COURTS

H M Advocate v McIntosh 2001 SLT 304; 2001 SCCR 1991; [2001] All ER 638; [2001] 3 WLR 107; [2001] 2 WLR 817

Olga Tellis & ORS v Bombay Municipal Corporation and Others (1985 INSG ISS, 10 July 1985)

Appendix 2

R v Lambert [2001] UKHL 37; [2002] 2 AC 545, [2001] 3 WLR 206

R v Secretary of State for Education and Employment and others ex parte Williamson and others [2005] UKHL 15, [2005] 2 AC 246, [2005] 2 WLR 590

Sauvé v Canada (Chief Electoral Officer)[2002] 3 SCR 519; 2002 SCC 68 (October 31, 2002)

Index

Index